new england's most intriguing gangsters, rascals, rogues, and thieves

By marc L. songini

covered Bridge press
north attleborough, ma

Copyright © 1998 by Marc L. Songini.

All Rights Reserved.

No part of this book may be reproduced by any means without written permission from the publisher.

Covered Bridge Press
7 Adamsdale Road
N. Attleborough, MA 02760
(508) 761-7721

Cover illustration by Wayne Geehan

Cover design by Don Langevin

Printed in the United States of America

First Edition

10 9 8 7 6 5 4 3 2 1

table of contents

Introduction	1
1. Thomas Morton, Quincy's Lord of Misrule	6
2. The Charming Joe Kennedy	25
3. Providence Godfather Raymond Patriarca	47
4. Jim Fisk, Vermont's Greatest Clown	87
5. The Pious Samuel Adams	107
6. Hetty Green, New England's Greatest Cheapskate	127
7. James Michael Curley: Boston's Robin Hood	141
8. The Intolerable Benedict Arnold	160
9. James "Whitey" Bulger, South Boston's Favorite Son	175
Bibliography	212

Dedication

To my father, a grand old rogue, who is no doubt looking up right now and watching with amusement (only kidding), and to JMO, who was a saint, and never knew it.

"History...is, indeed, little more than a register of the crimes, follies, and misfortunes of mankind."
—Gibbon

"The Devil is all for himself."
—Goethe, *Faust*

Introduction

What makes people evil? To paraphrase Shakespeare's character, Malvolio: "Some men are born crooked, others attain to crookedness, still others have crookedness thrust upon them."

This applies to the nine characters depicted in this book. They all, for various reasons, decided to engage in lives that broke the laws--both written and unwritten--of their times. Some were pirates of finance—Hetty Green and James Fisk, Jr.; others were outright gangsters who sometimes dabbled in legitimate business—James "Whitey" Bulger and Raymond L.S. Patriarca; others still were political felons—Thomas Morton, Benedict Arnold and James Michael Curley. And of course, there was Joseph Kennedy, who was all the above.

So, you might ask, what made these people so bad? It's a broad question that doesn't deserve a simple or single answer. Generally, however, an act that intentionally makes another person suffer is evil. However, does anyone ever think they are genuinely bad? I doubt it. If we compare ourselves to someone we consider evil, we usually discover that what separates us from them is our sense of what is right or wrong. And in the big picture, those things are determined by assessing a person's biology, family, surroundings, and experiences—and no two humans have exactly identical experiences. So, let us admit that evil is a somewhat loose state of being, and our subjects run the gamut from being merely naughty to downright diabolical.

How did I come to pick these nine among the many notable scoundrels nurtured in New England's rocky soil? It wasn't easy. In the final analysis, these were the most unusual, notorious and well-rounded characters; people who were interesting in and of themselves. They were all famous—at least in their times—and outrageous.

We must admit these people are intriguing. They broke the rules; they did what many of us would only dream of. Indeed, their willingness to impose their obnoxious selves on society despite heavy opposition is tough not to admire.

What's my own take on these people whom I have spent the last two years with on an intimate basis?

Although I have included two gangsters in here, I would like to state this book in not a celebration of their lifestyles or an attempt to glamorize or whitewash them. Too much fawning attention is given such men and while I have attempted to portray them as sympathetically and fairly as possible, I find next to nothing redeeming about them. Should of course I ever meet the famous Whitey Bulger, of course, which is not likely, I would be willing to get his side of the story. Even his brother's unwillingness to comment on him is well known, and I would be unable to resist any insight into this man.

I would also have to say I find the weirdest and least sympathetic of them to be Hetty Green, the miser and Wall Street magnate. While she possessed physical courage, which was accompanied by undoubted and genuine concern for people, she refused to assist them with money—or even raise her own lifestyle out of the level of extreme poverty. Though hugely wealthy, there is little to envy about her; her joyless life is more of a cautionary tale than anything else.

Of the characters, the most loveable was James Fisk Jr., who, though a thief, was personally generous, and was possessed of a boyishness that was irresistible. Fisk, however, may have caused more suffering than anyone else featured in this book; his idiotic and unbelievably greedy scheme to corner the gold market caused worldwide economic chaos—and is the best argument for regulating an economy as I have ever heard.

Despite his ill fame, Benedict Arnold is certainly the most brazenly courageous, and so dangerous of all the personalities in this book, and it's tough not to give him grudging admiration on this point. However, let us always remember that he betrayed men who themselves were traitors to their mother country.

Boston politician, James Michael Curley, has benefited a little too much from the notion that his willingness to take care of the poor excuses all his specious Brahmin-bashing and venality. He could have taken care of the poor and been less greedy at the same time and history would have been much kinder to him. But at the same time, Curley is an appealing character, and there is no doubt that many of his public works needed doing.

Samuel Adams, the Father of the American Revolution, despite the halo of patriotism hanging over his head, I personally disliked. His dishonesty and willingness to shed blood for a cause, which was never as oppressive as it was in his own violent imagination, does not recommend him well.

Joseph Kennedy, despite the cloud that hangs over his reputation, was not that unique—remember, he must be seen in the context of his environment, where treachery, Irish clannishness, back-stabbing and womanizing all walked easily hand in hand. The problem was that Kennedy lied so much and so successfully about his activities that, in exaggerative counterbalance, biographers now go out of their way to reveal just how bad he was.

Then there is Morton, whom I have included not because we think he was bad today, but because society, at least European society, in his time judged him harshly. Indeed, his humane treatment of Indians and indentured servants seems enlightened to us. That he gave guns to the Native Americans around him is only a blemish on his record if you believe that the whites were pre-ordained by God to own the continent and Indians only an impediment demanding as rapid removal as possible. Morton's only crime was not bowing down to the rising power of Plymouth, which regrettably defined much of how the New World would develop.

In terms of relative importance between these nine personalities, there are great gaps. Morton influenced few people in his time and made a bigger splash as a literary figure than a renegade. Although wealthy and successful, with a lot of power in the underworld and his immediate neighborhood, Patriarca had probably only as much influence as any wealthy, well connected corporate CEO, and in some ways, less. The same applies to James "Whitey" Bulger. In contrast, Hetty Green and Jim Fisk shook Wall Street as major financial players. However, despite his temporary effect on the politics of his time and his sons, Joe Kennedy had no lasting influence of his own in any field; the same is also true of Curley, who outlived nearly all his family, and saw none of them go on to any great achievements.

Scholars still debate just how crucial Benedict Arnold was in the American Revolutionary War battles he is most famous for; what is not debated was that his the story of his exploits gave the Americans more of a stomach to fight. Samuel Adams (who watched Arnold's feats closely), a small town political hack and stringpuller, has the right to the greatest kudos—after all he engineered both the Revolution and the Declaration of Independence.

The reader will also note that the various characters often touched on each other's lives—something possible only in a small region like New England. For instance, James Curley and Joe Kennedy rubbed shoulders in Boston politics, it was Kennedy's father, P.J., that made Curley mayor; later Joe Kennedy paid off Curley's debts and Curley vacated his congressional seat for Jack Kennedy to make his political start.

Raymond Patriarca, who may or may not have bumped into Kennedy during the bootlegging years of prohibition, faced down Robert Kennedy, who was counsel for a senate subcommittee investigating organized crime. Patriarca in turn knew Stevie Flemmi (whom he unsuccessfully tried to recruit for the Office), partner to Whitey Bulger.

One disclaimer: I am not a historian; I possess no special credentials except an excessive fascination with human weakness and vice. This is not a definitive reference resource on any of these characters. The collection is meant to do little more than entertain; if it whets the reader's appetite to explore the history of the region further, than it will have done more than I deserve or expect.

Introduction

A final note. While these people may be interesting, amusing and charming as individuals, we should not like them too much. The subjects enjoyed their lives and acts at the expense of various victims. Whether they were breaking the express, written laws of their time or flaunting the unwritten rules, they all did it at the expense of others.

I think it safe to say these people all suffered from an excess of self-love and a need for gratification at any cost, along with the conviction they were entitled to do as they pleased. Add to this an ability to lie, frighten, or convince others to obey them, and you have a successful scoundrel. And remember—it is society that creates these people and empowers them. Ultimately, we are to blame for them, as well.

Marc Songini

chapter one

thomas morton, quincy's lord of misrule

In June, 1628, New England's first lawman was waiting impatiently outside the cabin of its first criminal gang leader in Passonagessit, now called the city of Quincy. The policeman was the small, violent Miles Standish. He had nine soldiers with him, and they were all determined to get their quarry inside, Sir Thomas Morton, dead or alive. As far as Standish was concerned, preferably dead.

The posse had recently arrived from Plymouth Plantation with orders from its elders to arrest the rebel Morton, whom they called a "monster," and break up his settlement, which threatened the security of all the English in Massachusetts Bay.

However, Morton, drunk and heavily armed, had locked himself and two henchmen securely inside his log house. Captain Standish was no doubt nervous, as he was out of his territory and in Morton's "den," the settlement of Merry Mount.

Nevertheless, the murderous Standish's considerable capacity to hate sustained him. He had a personal vendetta against Morton—the "seven headed hydra" who had offended all of Massachusetts Bay by his many crimes and—even worse—by erecting a may pole, a symbol of carnal wickedness and an open insult to the holy colony at Plymouth. What was worse, Morton had just escaped from Standish and his troops the slip and made fools of them.

Standish' quarry was indeed a formidable opponent, the son of a soldier and a crack shot. Morton watched the men sent to arrest him outside through the portholes of his cabin, ready to shoot them down like so many geese. He wouldn't surrender to "Captain Shrimp," as he called the diminutive Standish, without a bloody fight. Nor was Standish going to leave unsuccessfully. The wait began, and so started the first "stand-off" in New England history.

Morton has a claim to fame as the father of organized crime in New England. He and his small band of drifters were the first recognized outlaw, or "underworld" gang in the region, later to be followed by the likes of Samuel Adams, Raymond Patriarca, and a host of other notable rogues.

When Morton was in his prime, the Puritan authorities considered him one of the most dangerous men in Massachusetts Bay and vented their considerable hate and power in crushing him. Their victory over him was short-lived. In the years that have elapsed since he died in Maine, Morton has been celebrated in poems, novels, and biographical treatments as something of a hero.

Many view his story as one of the few refreshing wafts of fresh air in the rigid, violent and closed history of Puritan society—a bit of Merrie Olde England transplanted to the severe new world, a Falstaff among theocratic Malvolios. Maybe so.

LIFE IN LONDON

We know little of his earliest years in England, except that he claimed the distinction of being a gentleman, was well educated and had powerful friends in the court of King Charles I. He also had the reputation of being a London "pettifogger," or shyster. He was witty, liked to read, and for amusement he associated with the hard-drinking and loose-living playwright Ben Jonson at the Mermaid Tavern; he may have even known Shakespeare.

His first recorded act of skullduggery dates back to 1621. Morton was representing a widow, the Dame Agnes Miller, who wanted to prevent her ne'er-do-well son from plundering her estate. Lawyer Morton wisely decided the estate was better squandered by a more mature man of educated tastes, and so married Dame Agnes himself.

After her death, Agnes' son decided he'd been had and started a lawsuit against Morton and won. However, the future

Lord of Misrule had by this time sold everything Dame Agnes had owned, including her "wearing apparel," and fled. Morton's son-in-law inherited an empty house.

Looking for a new life, Morton, in his 40s, took some money, perhaps from his wife's estate, and bought into a fur trading company destined for New England. There, in America, like many a man before and since, he hoped to become rich. He also possibly hoped to escape the reputation that he had exploited his late spouse. Other hints of crookedness hung over his head: probably around this time, a vague rumor began to spread that he had murdered a business partner, not a big revelation; life was indeed cheap in Elizabethan times.

In 1625, he arrived in Boston Harbor on the ship *Unity* with a Captain Wollaston, and thirty indentured servants and provisions. The vessel's name proved a misnomer, given the discord its passengers were about to cause in the New World. They planned to establish a plantation on what was then the edge of a very wide-open frontier that extended for an unlimited and unimagined distance.

The would be fur-traders built their outpost, Mount Wollaston, at Passonagessit (Quincy), an attractive area set in the midst of low wooded hills, marshlands, and open grassy fields. They were not far from Plymouth Plantation, established some years before by Puritans, whose rigid theocratic code was soon to bring them in collision with their new neighbors.

BRAVE NEW WORLD

After three years passed without making the hoped-for profits that had brought him there, Captain Wollaston decided enough was enough. He headed south, bringing most of his servants with him. He auctioned these men, whose status was just above that of slaves, to Virginia planters. An unlucky man named Fitcher was left as "lieutenant" in charge at Passonagessit.

Morton, however, full of hope that he could make a fortune here and attracted to the rugged beauty of the land and its natural wealth of crops, game, and space, had decided to stay—a turning point in his life.

Ever the egoist, he soon arrived at the conclusion that everyone would be st served if he became the new master of Mount Wollaston. But he was at this time a nobody in the camp, and that had to be changed. First, he threw a feast, complete with "some strong drink" that made the half dozen remaining servants at the plantation "merry."

When the servants were softened up with alcohol, Morton made his pitch. "You see," he said, "that many of your fellows are carried to Virginia. And if you stay....you will also be carried away and sold for slaves with the rest. Therefore, I would advise you to thrust out this Lieutenant Fitcher."

He promised the revelers he would make them free men and take them in as his partners in the plantation. Morton was something of a democrat, promising his listeners that "we will converse, trade, plant and live together as equals, and support and protect one another."

While Morton was not exactly being altruistic, his words found a ready home in the imaginations of the dispossessed servants. His "counsell was easily received," and Fitcher was out. Expelled from Mount Wollaston into the wilds with nothing, the hapless lieutenant had to beg his bread from other neighboring settlers until he could get passage back to England.

Morton, now first amongst equals, soon changed the plantation's name from Mount Wollaston to one more to his liking: "Merry Mount," a pun on the Latin phrase, "Mare Mount," or "Mountain by the Sea." Being a contemporary of word master Shakespeare, he may also have had a third sexual pun in mind, particularly given the activities going on there with the accommodating local Indian women.

And the women did come, along with their men, with whom Morton set up a brisk and successful fur trade, using two commodities very attractive to Native Americans—guns and liquor. A successful enterprise launched, the inhabitants of Merry Mount began enjoying a lifestyle that was a stunning contrast to that of their church-going Puritan neighbors a few miles south in Plymouth.

Left to their own devices, Morton, the worldly Elizabethan swashbuckler, and his gang of ex-servants did what came naturally to men with no women or law to police them. Living by the strict code of Leviticus (the harsh book of laws in the Old Testament) as the Puritans did, never seemed to have crossed their minds. They drank and fornicated in earnest, and it is to their dubious credit the gang of Merry Mount—unlike many other Europeans in the New World—didn't consider itself too good to bed with the native women.

As William Bradford, Governor of Plymouth Plantation and Morton's mortal enemy put it, they "fell to great licentiousness and led a dissolute life" venturing into "all profaneness." There was little love lost or to lose between a man like Morton and the Puritans; back in England the public shunned the Puritans as cruel and intolerant zealots; the sect was also at odds with the king. Unpopular and undesirable, and driven from country to country, it was only in America where the Puritans found not freedom from persecution, but rather the freedom to persecute others without interference.

To the excitable Bradford, Morton became the "Lord of Misrule" who, horror of horrors, was maintaining a virtual "school of atheism."

Morton became wealthy trading with the local Indians, but spent most of his money keeping himself and his band of merry men in "wine and strong waters" which they drank "in great excess"—some $500 worth each morning, said Bradford. Whether Morton was trying to keep his followers happily docile or just found drunkenness a desirable state of being or both is unclear.

Pleased with his new role as master of ceremonies in the New World, he began to call himself "Mine Host." He had arrived home. Unlike the city bred and bound Puritans of Plymouth, the country dweller Morton could play the roving woodsman and gentleman, hunting with his dog or fishing as he had in England. He developed a great love of New England and its rugged landscape. He gloried in its natural beauties, and even claimed that Merry Mount's water could cure "melancholy." He prefigured Thoreau by two centuries.

THE ABOMINATION

Believing the plantation would be a "memorial to after ages," says Morton, the gang marked the establishment of the settlement with a formal christening, complete "with revels and merriment after the old English custom." The event coincided with May Day—an old pagan holiday celebrating sexual indulgence which was commonly observed wherever Englishmen were—unless, of course, they were Puritans, who thought it evil.

The party lasted days. They opened a barrel of "excellent beer" with "other good drink" to quench their considerable thirst for alcohol. The sound of singing, drumbeats, and the explosion of muskets and pistols rang in the wilderness. Morton, less a racist by far than the Puritans, even allowed the "Savages" (as the Indians were called), who had come out to see what the ruckus was about, to take part in the May Day celebration.

The Englishmen, as their custom was, took the Native American women as "consorts." As Morton's song went: "Lasses in beaver coats come away, ye shall be welcome to us night and day."

The centerpiece of the party was the erection of a Maypole, 80 feet long, on a hill that had a commanding view of the countryside for miles around. So tall was the pole it could serve as a "sea mark," said Morton; crowning the pole were a pair of buck's horns. Maypoles were popular with Englishmen, and perhaps he felt a bit nostalgic at recapturing a piece of his homeland in the new world.

The liquor kept flowing, while one celebrant recited a song Morton had written with the lines: "Drink and be merry, merry, merry boys." As the song echoed in the hills, the revelers, white and red men both, danced hand in hand.

Morton, a writer of sexual verse, also wrote a long poem to commemorate the occasion and affixed it to the Maypole. The work itself was designed to confuse and annoy the "Separatists," as he called the Puritans. Like the famous modern poem, the "Waste Land," Morton's work is virtually meaningless without endless footnotes. Nevertheless, Morton felt he had started a tradition. The poem's closing lines read : "With proclamation that the first of May/At Mar-e Mount shall be kept holiday."

With his insults to Plymouth, Morton had outdone himself this time; he had in effect, asked his enemies to crush him. As he himself later admitted, the erection of the May pole "was a lamentable spectacle to the precise separatists....They termed it an idol...the Calf of Horeb."

This "harmless mirth" was an attack directly on the Puritan way of life; the Separatists renamed Merry Mount to Mount Dagon, in reference to the Biblical place of idolatry. Revenge was assured. As Mine Host put it, the Puritans threatened to change it from a Merry Mount to a "woeful mount." His enemies spent time "troubling their brains more than reason would require." Morton, the gentleman hedonist, had no grasp of the Puritans' hatred of pleasure.

It probably only had a matter of time, but with the erection of the Maypole, the Puritans decided things were truly getting out of hand. Bradford said that it had been as if "they had anew revived and celebrated...the beastly practices of the mad Bacchanalians." Bradford was also incensed about Morton's poem, which he knew had been written as an insult to his sect; not only that, it tended to "lasciviousness."

The Lord of Misrule, "thinking himself lawless" and caring only to "maintain this riotous prodigality and profuse excess " now began flooding the Indians with guns. Morton also taught them his hunting techniques sent them out to shoot game for him.

The Indians "became mad" to get as many guns as they could any way they could, said Bradford. Morton "having thus taught them the uses of pieces sold them all he could spare." The demand outran the supply and Morton and his company had to order more from England.

The stern governor bewailed "the mischief that this wicked man began." Firearms in the hands of Indians were dangerous—they equalized the balance of power in the New World. That was intolerable to men such as Bradford, who were trying to create the new Zion, or holy land, on the coast of North America and wanted to get rid of the Savages as soon as possible. He noted that these armed Indians were beginning to murder colonists and held other settlers in their mercy. Morton's sinful trade with the Indians was dulling the Englishmen's edge.

"O, the horribleness of this villainy!" bewailed Bradford, who considered Morton to be a greedy murderer. Morton's smaller neighbors were also terrified that the trade in guns would continue and the Indians would kill them.

Bradford, who like all Englishmen was obsessed to preserve his place on the social ladder, feared Merry Mount would became a nest of "discontents" where "the scum of the country... would flock." He feared Plymouth's servants would flee and join the all-embracing Morton; there could be an outbreak of democracy.... This nest of vipers would eventually become more dangerous than the Indians themselves.

The worst part of it, no doubt, was that Morton was a success. He was making good of it in the new land. A pest like him had to be removed and an example made. They had to stop the Lord of Misrule and his "consorts" before they grew even more powerful. But like the patient and calculating spider that he was, the shrewd Bradford bided his time before overwhelming his fly.

THE PURITANS STRIKE

A year after the Maypole's erection, the Plymouth elders, along with the other smaller settlers from along the coast from Nantasket to Maine, decided in spring 1628 to temporarily put aside their hate for one another, and sent the "wicked" Morton a "friendly and neighborly" letter.

Morton, an Anglican who considered the Puritans vicious fanatics, treated the admonishment with scorn. He was a gentleman who wanted life's pleasures and to do as he saw fit. He refused to take commands from anyone else. He believed, with good reason, the Puritans envied his prosperity and only wanted him out of the way so they could increase their own profits in the lucrative fur trade.

The coalition issued another letter, claiming the king had issued a proclamation banning selling guns to the Indians. Morton said "the king's proclamation was no law" and asked "what penalty was on it?" He saw through the communications, and threatened the Puritans that he would be ready for anyone sent to "molest" him.

The Puritans decided it was now time to change tactics— they realized there was no way to deal with so proud and independent a man as the Lord of Misrule "but to take him by force." The elders collected money was collected and prepared to send a military party off.

In June, Captain Miles Standish, the military protector and bully of Plymouth, left the plantation to stop this threat to safety, orthodoxy and prosperity. This small homicidal man, a one-time drummer (as Morton contemptuously noted) and mercenary, had a great talent for violence. Once he had summarily hanged seven Indians at Wessagusset (Weymouth) merely because he suspected them of being hostile.

This was the man, who with his party, planned to destroy Morton and torch his house.

However, when the party arrived at Merry Mount, Morton was away at another settlement in Wessagussett, unsuspecting the posse was after him. Standish' troop pursued and located and arrested him nevertheless. As Morton put it, they "set upon my honest host....And they charged him....with criminal things. " Morton considered these accusations a mere "gloss upon their malice." They wanted him out of the way so they could make more money in furs.

Standish' party was overjoyed at the easy bagging of their "capital enemy" and "fell to tippling." Mine Host pretended to be sad and refused to eat or drink with his captors—or the nine "worthies" as he ironically called them. Morton kept up the charade until he had the chance to "give them a slip," although six men were left to watch him—one of them even lying with him in bed as extra measure.

Drunk, the party didn't notice as Morton crept off his bed and out from the room he was lying in. He passed through first one door...then a second one that led outside. He unlocked the outer door quietly....then, on his way out, he could not resist slamming it behind him loudly. The drunken soldiers awoke and found their prisoner....gone! Morton heard a ruckus behind him:

"Oh, he's gone! What shall we do? He's gone!" they cried. Everyone jumped up and ran around in the dark, the soldiers slammed into each other head-on. "Their grand leader, Captain Shrimp," said the amused Morton, was beside himself. Standish "tore his clothes for anger." The Worthies, who cropped their heads closely, were so angry they would have torn out their hair if it had been long enough, claimed Mine Host.

CAPTURE AND TRIAL

A thunderstorm began. Morton ran on in the night, flashes of lightning briefly lighting his path. The scene was idiotic. He made it back the few miles to Merry Mount where he had his cache of weapons and two of his men. Locking his door, he got ready for a fight.

Morton would have fit in well with the members of the modern back-to-nature gun movement particularly as represented by the National Rifle Association. Merry Mount was something of a fort, well provisioned for combat. Morton took out three pounds of powder, four "good guns" for himself and his two assistants, and bullets of "several sizes." He gathered a considerable amount of liquor, and got very drunk, possibly to steady his nerves.

His enemies were in fast pursuit, with the red-faced, red-haired Standish, "the first captain in the land," hungry to redress Morton's insulting escape. Soon, he arrived at Merry Mount with his eight Worthies demanding surrender. The "stand-off" began.

Cannily, at first Standish at first offered to make a deal with Morton, and let him keep his guns and allow himself to be deported back to England. But, as Bradford later, said "they could get nothing but scoffs and scorns from him."

The hunted man considered through the haze of alcohol the terms offered; decided he'd rather surrender then shed blood and possibly lose to the greater numbers arrayed against him. He told Standish, however, "no violence should be offered to his person." Standish agreed.

The door opened and Mine Host and his men appeared, armed. Immediately, Standish leaped with his Worthies on their quarry so violently it seemed they wanted to literally devour him. After the scuffle, Morton was a prisoner again. No one was seriously hurt, but one of Mine Host's men, drunk, clumsily ran into someone's sword and impaled his own nose.

Ironically, if Morton had pulled the trigger of his carbine, it might very well have been his last shot. The weapon, which he had loaded while intoxicated, was overcharged—half-stuffed with powder and shot, and would have exploded in his face.

In any case, following what he called an "outrageous riot," Mine Host was now in his enemy's power. Standish and his band plundered Merry Mount, then took their prisoner down to Plymouth to be judged.

At Morton's trial, Standish spoke up to urge them to execute the prisoner. He couldn't see why any more time should be wasted on the Lord of Misrule. Indeed, if they sent Morton back to England, then he, Standish planned to shoot Morton with his pistol as they loaded him aboard ship for deportation.

For whatever reason, the Plymouth elders were wary of executing Morton; perhaps they feared his influence, certainly they didn't act out of humanity. The elders decided—with their typical Puritan charity—to allow Morton to live, but take away everything he owned and leave him on the bleak and desolate Isles of Shoals off the Maine coast, with nothing but the clothes on his back and let him face the winter. It was, in effect, a long, slow and lonely death sentence.

But if the Puritans had indeed planned Morton would starve or freeze to death, they were wrong. The local Indians canoed out to the island and brought Morton, whom they considered "the sachem of Passonagessit," provisions, including liquor. A "league of brotherhood" formed between the Savages and Mine Host, as Morton realized, as many historians were to later, that the Indians were in some ways more "full of humanity" than the so-called Christians. After a month passed, Morton shipped back to England, full of complaints for the authorities there.

MINE HOST RETURNS

In his native land, Morton, the successful courtier, did not receive "so much as a rebuke" from the authorities. However, in his absence, things changed at Merry Mount. That fall, Puritan John Endicott, an intolerant fanatic second to none, came overseas with permission to found the colony of Massachusetts Bay, which included Merry Mount. On inspecting the site of "Mount Dagon," he ordered the Maypole cut down. Endicott then "rebuked" Morton's company for their "profaneness" and told them to "look there should be better walking."

It seemed Morton was defeated. God had delivered the Puritans' enemy into their hands, and they breathed with relief. But they hadn't reckoned on the tenacity and spirit of their gentleman opponent. In 1629, almost unbelievably, Mine Host returned—not just to New England, but to Plymouth itself, as a guest of a man named Allerton—setting mouths agape. The locals felt that Allerton, a businessman, had offered them a "great and just offense...in bringing...for base gaine, that unworthy man, Morton." Allerton not only brought the hated man back over, but took him into their town and employed him as a "scribe."

Morton was a man of spirit indeed. It is easy to forget that the Puritans were dangerous to cross, prone to deal with their enemies by branding them or cutting off their ears when they didn't just hang them outright. But apparently, the cheeky Lord of Misrule didn't care, nor was he afraid of the opinion of the crowd. Nevertheless, the Puritans eventually forced Allerton to drive Morton out of the plantation.

This expulsion was no great tragedy to the Lord of Misrule, who went back to his "old nest" in Massachusetts Bay. There he returned to his sins with liquor, weapons, and Indians. As he was out of the Plymouth jurisdiction, Bradford could fume, but do nothing about it—unlike the even harsher Endicott.

Soon after, the Massachusetts authorities summoned Morton to Salem for a general assembly. Trying to legislate his own peculiar version of morality, Endicott demanded the assembly sign a document containing articles that would instruct everyone on how to "follow the rule of God's word."

Those who broke the rules faced expulsion from the colony. Morton the lawyer probably sniffed a trap that would get him thrown out of New England again. The shrewd councilor and agent of the king's faction agreed only to sign if the articles also said "so as nothing be done contrary" to the laws of England. He stopped Endicott right there, and won his point. However, he made no friends over it.

The assembly also decided to monopolize the fur trade by forcing everyone to join and invest in one newly created company. Morton weaseled out of it, but those who invested in the company lost their money. Morton "derided the Contributors for being catch'd in that snare." He was making some 700 percent in profit, so he didn't need to link his fortunes with anyone.

ARRESTED AGAIN

Endicott finally sent a party to arrest Morton; the Lord of Misrule got news of the posse and fled. The commissioners sent to arrest him found a house empty except for corn, which they ate, leaving only a small morsel "for mine Host to keep Christmas with." Without food, Morton took to the woods and hunted to fill his stomach, laughing long and loud at Endicott—who was too busy fighting starvation and plague in colony to do anything about it.

Endicott's successor, John Winthrop, started the attack on Morton again, issuing yet another warrant. This time the puritans caught their quarry and assaulted him with a trumped up charge. Showing an unusual concern for the rights of the race they were destroying, the Puritans charged Morton with stealing an Indian's canoe. It was absurd.

"And now Mine Host must suffer," Morton noted. Indeed. Court convened in Charlestown, and Winthrop sentenced Morton to be first put in the bilboes (stocks). Next, that his goods should all be confiscated, and his plantation be burned to the ground (the Puritans didn't want "the habitation of the wicked" to be in "Israel" any longer). Lastly, they banished him.
The authorities carried out the sentence quickly and with relish.

As the boat carrying Morton home left the coastline of Massachusetts, the Puritans burnt the Lord of Misrule's house while he watched. It was a vicious touch that the Puritans were so apt at performing. Morton said the ascending smoke was like that from the polluted sacrifice of the murderer Cain in the book of Genesis. He said "nothing did remain but the bare ashes." On the ride home on the ship *Handmaid*, he nearly starved, as the authorities had intended. He later claimed his treatment was fit for a "man worthy of death." Things did not improve in England, and when he arrived in port, he landed in jail.

A BITTER ENEMY

Now the Puritans had a real enemy to contend with. Over the next decade, Morton began working for Sir Ferdinando Gorges, a member of the Council of New England. This committee, established by and for the king, oversaw the new colonies and was bound to conflict with the Puritans and their settlements. Gorges was himself enemy of the Separatists and planned to oust them and take the region for himself.

Looking to curry favor with the English court, now Morton absurdly claimed the Puritans' persecution of him was because he was a member of the Church of England. He claimed the Puritans had persecuted him not because of his trade in guns or liquor or his jollity but for his use of the Anglican *Book of Common Prayer*, a volume the Puritans shunned. Ever the lawyer, he devised intricate legal challenges for the Puritans to wriggle out of. His work was not completely unsuccessful—in 1634, he announced with glee that the patent, or permission, given to the Massachusetts Bay Colony had been revoked and a new royal governor was coming; the Puritans in Massachusetts began to fortify Boston harbor in case of war with mother England.

"Repent you cruel Separatists, repent," Morton wrote.

He didn't limit his attacks to the courtroom. Morton began work on a book that took its place as an early piece of North American literature, the *New English Canaan*. It was an outright attack on the Puritans of New England; Bradford claimed it "full of lies and slanders."

In it Morton paints an uneven but sometimes moving portrait of the New World, the lay of the land, its inhabitants. Some of the book is accurate. One thing that does shine to Mine Host's credit, even for his critics, is the appreciation he had for the land had fallen in love with.

"I did not think that in all the known world it could be paralleled for so many goodly groves of trees, dainty fine round rising hillocks, delicate fair large plains, sweet crystal fountains, and clear running streams that twine in fine meanders through the meads [meadows], making so sweet a murmuring noise to hear as would even lull the senses with delight asleep...." says Morton. He called New England "Nature's masterpiece" and declared: "If this land be not rich, then is the whole world poor."

We can laugh now at his speculations; he believed, for instance, the Indians descended from the survivors of the mythical city of Troy. Still a bit of a racist, he also claimed that God had cleared out most of the Indians with disease so the European Christians could use their land. He declared the diseased decimation of the Natives as a sign of the "wondrous wisdom and love God."

Morton hoped to return with the blessing of Gorges and the king to be governor of Massachusetts. For this, he waited ten years for nothing. His testimony in court against the Puritans only won Gorges a reprimand.

A CRAZY OLD MAN

In 1643, Morton, now quite old, sealed his will and yet again returned to New England. He appeared near Duxbury hunting, outraging Miles Standish, who had founded the town and couldn't stand the idea that the Lord of Misrule was "a-fowling in his ground."

However, Morton had the protection of Gorges and claimed to be the agent of powerful Puritans back in England. Morton was actually Gorges' spy, attempting to gather enough evidence against the Puritans to have the king revoke their charters. Had Gorges been more effective a schemer, and had the bloodthirsty and cruel Puritan dictator Oliver Cromwell not seized power in the mother country, Morton might have had his way.

However, Morton, now old, weak and decrepit, resorted to going around flashing an envelope with an official seal on it, indicating his mighty but mythical sponsors. Nevertheless, he was still a hated man; as one enemy, said he was the "odium of our people" and one of the "arrantest" known knaves "that ever trod on New English shore." (Street crime does not pay: such relentless treatment greeted Raymond Patriarca and Whitey Bulger in their old age, also.)

One man noted that Morton "cannot procure the least respect amongst our people." He had no money, and lived off water—which no one drank in those years— instead of beer and other spirits.

With his characteristic doggedness, Morton kept hunting in Standish's territory, the murderous captain threatening to shoot him all the while. Morton apparently had not yet given up on intrigue; in 1644 he decided to join up with a party of men loyal to the king who were based in Maine. He started on his way north through Gloucester when he caught the attention of a Puritan Captain, John Endicott.

Endicott told governor Winthrop, rather imaginatively, he suspected Morton was working for the Jesuits "to do us mischief." The authorities issued a warrant, but Morton eluded his pursuers.

He appeared next in Rhode Island, where he started putting out feelers to see who would support the king. He disclosed there would be rewards for supporters of Charles I, and when Gorges came, Morton would take back the lands promised him. Morton insinuated he "knew whose roasts his spits and jacks turned."

While he was trying to make his way back up to Maine through Massachusetts, the Puritans caught him and claimed Morton was trying to incite the crown to destroy their settlements. This of course was true. In September, they accused him of charging them with treason and rebellion. When he went to Boston for trial, Morton's defense was he had only been a witness in court proceedings against the Puritans—not the instigator of them.

The Puritans may have known Morton was lying, but didn't care. It was war. They jailed him for six months while seeking evidence against him from England—which never came.

While awaiting indictment, the proud cavalier Morton broke. He asked the member of the General Court to "cast back your eyes and behold what your poor petitioner had suffered." He said that he was a "poor worm" who wanted to crawl out of his condition; he complained of "the decaying of his limbs."

One of the two magistrates hearing his plea was Major Edward Gibbons, one of his former gang at Merry Mount. Gibbons had become a successful man among the Puritans, and the plight of his former comrade meant nothing to him now, so he let Morton sit in jail another six months.

At last the magistrates decided come to some sort of verdict and fined Morton 100 pounds (about $5,000) and released him. So feeble and miserable was the old man, not even the vengeful Puritans, whose ability to hate was considerable, bothered to inflict any more suffering on the one time Lord of Misrule.

"He was a charge to the country, for he had nothing," said Winthrop, "and we thought not to fit corporal punishment upon him, being old and crazy...." They gave him his liberty—that is, liberty to starve and freeze in the wilds of New England. Morton couldn't pay the fine and the Puritans knew this; this was unspoken invitation to leave their colony and not come back.

So Morton the wanderer hit the road once again and found his way to the small royalist outpost of Agamenticus (now called York), Maine, where the winters are harsh, and the coastline rugged and rocky. He lived there two years, an impoverished despised old man. In 1647, the stress of his destitution, hardships and imprisonment got to him and his health broke and he died in obscurity.

There were no family or friends in America to mourn him. His less than charitable contemporaries considered him a pathetic old fool better off dead than alive—and they may have had a point, given the low state he had fallen into.

So, thus passed Thomas Morton: scribbler of mediocre verse, sportsman, lawyer, schemer, spy, gun-runner, drunkard, fornicator and general rogue. Morton left virtually nothing behind him except the contempt of his enemies, broken dreams of wealth and land ownership, a book that would become one of the foundations of North American literature, and a legend that has never stopped growing in the past three centuries.

Literary giants such as Nathaniel Hawthorne and poets Robert Lowell and Henry Wadsworth Longfellow have retold his story. To some, he represents an alternate vision of the new world—a man who loved the wilderness and didn't need to live in a fortress like the Puritans in Plymouth. He was instead a man who loved the countryside he had grown up in. The Puritans, on the other hand, were originally city dwellers and feared the wilderness around them and wanted to subjugate the rugged forests and its inhabitants.

Morton, by and large, unlike his enemies, was also man enough to see that the broken scattered Native Americans were human beings and could be tolerated—and even befriended. The Puritans' racism and exploitation of the Indians eventually led to King Philip's War, a defining point in North American history; after that genocidal conflict, Native Americans were shunned and despised as powerless, fit only for destruction as the white races took what God had ordained them to have. That trend continues until this very day all over this continent.

Yet if Morton could have lived to see it, he might have found comfort to know that within the century Merry Mount's rivals, Plymouth Plantation and Massachusetts Bay, would be absorbed into what became the Commonwealth of Massachusetts.

Had Morton, for all his sins, became one of the defining founders of the New World, there might have been a far different history to write. Then again, perhaps not—but at least one thing is certain: with his defiance and willingness to break whatever rule suited him, all New England rogues and crooks can look at Morton as being their spiritual grandfather.

chapter two

the charming joe kennedy

One day in April, 1938, a flamboyant tycoon from Massachusetts of questionable—if any—business and sexual ethics found himself America's ambassador to the Court of St. James—that is, of England. That businessman, Joseph P. Kennedy, had indeed risen to the heights: an Irish Catholic was now the representative of the mightiest country in the world. Dressing in Windsor Castle for a dinner later with the King and Queen of England and Prime Minister Neville Chamberlain, Kennedy observed shrewdly to his wife: "Well, Rose, this is a hell of a long way from East Boston."

Shortly afterward, the British intelligence service, M-1, would "bug" him and record his pro-Nazi conversations; the local papers would denounce his defeatism and cowardice; and his former patron, President Franklin Roosevelt would destroy him politically and he would return home with his political dreams smashed.

Ultimately, Kennedy found that the road back to East Boston was the same as the road from it, and more quickly covered on the return voyage. Yet, Joseph Patrick Kennedy was one of the most promising and influential rascals ever to be nurtured in New England's environs—no small feat. It was not only by what he did in his own lifetime—but by his great invention: the Kennedy family. This creation, if nothing else, provides endless entertainment and vicarious satisfaction for the bored masses of America, desperately hungry for glamour, scandals and the need to denounce immorality.

Kennedy, the politician turned Hollywood mogul, eventually, with his family, turned Hollywood into politics.

He had many lives, in fact. Bootlegger, womanizer, cutthroat, kingmaker, diplomat, administrator, financial genius, movie mogul, passionate idealist for peace (or appeasement), loving father, liar—all these things and more was Kennedy. For good or bad, he and the family he made have had an influence on America and much of the world—at least symbolically.

Forests have been devoured to make the paper to print the books on the Kennedy saga. However, the treatments of Kennedy and his numerous progeny tend to swallow up his humanity and completely demonize him. This is just not fair. When he wanted, like most scoundrels, he had vast charm; he also had a very acute and Irish sense of humor—biting, savage, direct, and dark.

For instance, when one student of psychology from Princeton mailed Kennedy a questionnaire asking what was the secret of his financial success, the no-nonsense millionaire answered bluntly: "I am rich because I have a lot of money."

Kennedy was almost a force of nature; his energies and ambitions were huge; earning and stealing money came unusually easy to him, and morality in the ordinary—if any—sense of the word was meaningless. His feats were impressive. One must doff one's ward-heeler bowler to him: without any great talents except for lying, string-pulling, and cunning, he made it to the national—indeed, international—stage with his act.

NOT SO MODEST BEGINNINGS

But then again, he did have a step up; he had the right instincts inherited from his crooked politician father. He grew up in the Boston of felon Mayor Curley; he learned firsthand the Hibernican politician's arts of two-facedness and treachery, honed in generations of clan warfare in Ireland then further sharpened in the smoke filled back rooms and pubs of the "New World."

Eventually Kennedy brought his Boston-bred shenanigans to a glorious consummation in the presidency of his son, John—

whose administration's lies, deceit and cheap glitter are the fascination of the nation.

Kennedy was in born in the Irish enclave of East Boston, the grandson of an Irish tenant farmer. His father, Patrick Joseph Kennedy, a sometime saloonkeeper and an influential and crooked state legislator, overseer of utilities, and banker. Despite Kennedy's later claims of dire poverty, his family was rich and powerful and he grew up in a mansion a privileged, adored son with servants to attend him. Yet Kennedy didn't want just more for himself and his family—he wanted the most he could get legally—or otherwise. He was born to an era of conspicuous consumption; of great fortunes, of smokestack industries, of larger than life robber barons such as J.P. Morgan and Cornelius Vanderbilt, men who didn't care much about how they built their fortunes, or who they exploited and crushed. Joseph Kennedy imitated and even exceeded these role models, never once letting the human costs enter his balance sheets.

The freckle-faced, red haired boy with the cool blue eyes was on the make early on, starting work at twelve, delivering hats to the wealthy Brahmin women of Boston. Later, he sold candy and newspapers. The incipient anti-Semite even took tips for lighting the stoves of Orthodox Jews on their holy days. He was also something of a young impresario, directing plays in his backyard, for which he charged admission, although judging by the bad movies he later produced, this early foray into theater didn't give him much insight into art.

Although he later claimed he started out at the bottom, Kennedy was actually always on the track of privilege. He entered the prestigious Boston Latin High School, learning to speak like a Brahmin prince. A good athlete, he won the mayor's cup for the most outstanding batting average in the city. His future father-in-law and whipping boy, Boston mayor John "Honey Fitz" Fitzgerald presented him with the award. Kennedy was to turn even the National Pastime to his advantage, becoming founder, coach and manager of a baseball team called the Assumptions.

His motto: "If you can't be captain, don't play."

Continuing on the rise ever upward from money and influence to more money and influence, the tall, good-looking young man with the hard jaw and steely eyes entered Harvard as an "untouchable," as the Irish were called in that WASP reserve. His grades at Boston Latin had been poor, and it's probable Harvard accepted him only because of his influential father's intervention.

Kennedy was a dismal scholar at Harvard, had to drop a finance class, and probably secured his passage through the college by bribing his professors with bottles of expensive Scotch. Although, like his father P.J., Kennedy neither smoked nor drank, he did recognize the value of greasing the right palms with whatever would work. Despite his heritage and bad marks, he participated in the prestigious and exclusive Hasty Pudding Club.

His high profile skullduggery began while still a student. As a graduating senior, to get his athlete's letter, he pulled some strings (as he would do ad infinitum for the rest of his life) and stood in as first baseman in the final few moments of the Harvard-Yale game. Catching the ball that ended the game, instead of handing it to the pitcher out of courtesy, as expected, Kennedy walked off with it himself.

THE RISE TO SUCCESS

Now he was ready to begin his career as businessman. He was already making money, having used political influence to snag the rights to run a tour bus operation in Boston.

Although cunning and quick, Kennedy was not unusually intelligent. Physically, he had a delicate constitution. He was high strung, sensitive to criticism, and bullying; he struggled with neuritis and an ulcer most of his life. He had solid (although undeserved) educational credentials behind him, extensive political connections, and the good fortune not to be encumbered by a conscience to slow him down.

Yet, it is worth noting here that Kennedy was not, as some of his more hostile biographers have claimed, amoral. His ethics were indeed rather simple: much the product of the Irish clan system, he lived for his himself and his family, in that order—anything else was of secondary, if any, importance.

Despite his bad grades in finance, Kennedy decided to work in the money industry—not as a poor bank clerk but, through his father's connections, as state bank examiner. In retrospect, this was something like making Jack the Ripper the dean of a girl's boarding school. Kennedy not only learned the interior workings of the banking industry, even better, he discovered much about the confidential operations of many companies throughout the state. He worked a variety of jobs—later lying on his resume about the length of his tenure in them and eventually, a golden opportunity fell into his lap (well, actually, he nudged it slightly).

The Columbia Trust, a neighborhood bank, was about to fall victim to a takeover from a larger downtown bank. The Boston Irish felt they were going to lose a landmark institution. Kennedy, who cared little about the Irish community and a lot about money and advancement, stepped in to make his first play as a local champion.

He borrowed enough cash, much from his family, to buy enough of Columbia's stock to bluff the hostile bank to stop its takeover attempt. With father P.J.'s help, the directors of Columbia made the 25-year-old Kennedy the youngest (according to Kennedy) bank president in the country. Kennedy, despite his later wealth, never bothered to repay many of his creditors for their generosity in his first deal—even those who were related.

Career established, now came the next step up: marriage.

A MARRIAGE MADE IN HEAVEN

After meeting her at Old Orchard Beach, Maine, Kennedy began courting the most unattainable Irish maiden in the city: Rose Fitzgerald, mayor Honey Fitz' daughter. Allegedly, Kennedy had to do this on the sly, as "Honey" Fitz was not sweet on the notion of P.J. Kennedy's son winning his daughter—P.J. had been a fierce political rival of his.

But for young Joe, the attraction was overwhelming. Not only was Rose was pious, well educated, and pretty, she was also the daughter of the most powerful man in Boston and thus the Commonwealth of Massachusetts; it is still an open question whether or not Kennedy was romancing Rose or her father.

Although Kennedy said he considered girls "less than human" (a view that seems to prevail somewhat amongst the Kennedy males even to this day), with charm, attention, and endless flattery he was able to successfully stalk his prey, and married Rose on October 7, 1914.

The Boston cardinal himself presided over the wedding, which drew a small crowd. The social climbing Kennedy never forgot Honey Fitz' snubs; not much prone to forgiveness, Kennedy eventually repaid his father in law a thousandfold with insults and cruelty.

(This of course did not stand in the way of their political collaboration. In 1918, Kennedy helped mastermind Fitzgerald's crooked and successful run for congress—a victory later overturned by vote of the House of Representatives.)

Seeking a dynasty, Kennedy began producing children at an astonishingly rapid rate, even for that pre-birth control era, with Joseph Patrick Kennedy Jr.'s birth coming on July 28, 1915. Kennedy spent little time with his ever-expanding family, however, and rather concentrated on making money and cheating on Rose. Far from being discrete about his fornication, Kennedy outdid himself to display his infidelities publicly often appearing openly with attractive women. Indeed, Kennedy's long hours at the bank were often a cover for his philandering. He had a simple motto he passed on to his sons: "A day without a lay is a day wasted."

Rose had a simple way of coping with her husband's tomcatting: she quietly ignored it with as much grace as she could muster, relying on the Rosary, conspicuous consumption, and prescription drugs to support her. She eventually withdrew almost completely from her family.

THE WAR, STOCK MARKET, AND BOOTLEGGING

World War I broke out. Physical courage—or patriotism—not being his strong suit, Kennedy avoided the draft and, as he would do later, used the conflict to raise his fortunes yet higher—and hide from combat. In 1917, although he knew nothing about shipbuilding, he—as usual—pulled some political strings and took a job as general manager of the Fore River shipyards in Quincy. He stayed mostly behind a desk where he could do the least damage to the normal operations of the facility.

Kennedy made an epic blunder almost immediately by refusing to honor an agreement made by the previous director of the shipyard to raise the wages of the shipyard's laborers. He thus forced the workers to strike; then-Assistant of the Secretary of the Navy Franklin D. Roosevelt stepped in the middle and smoothed the situation over, getting the laborers their money.

Kennedy, looking like a fool, later lied about his error, claiming the real confrontation had been over two destroyers that hadn't been paid for and that Roosevelt had taken by force. Kennedy, lying, dubbed the future president a "smiling four flusher." (His assessment was probably accurate, but as the saying goes, it takes one to know one.)

With the end of World War I, Kennedy no longer needed to hide from the draft, and so, like many others, entered the investment firm of Hayden, Stone and from there, the stock market, which at the time was about as regulated as the Wild West of legend. This was where he was to become rich, using every dirty trick in the book—and some outside the book as well. He knew the tactics of the swindler's trade—insider information; creating phony investment pools to artificially inflate the stock, then dumping it; artificially driving a company's stock down to defraud its investors...and so on.

It was his bizarre habit to turn on his friends and sponsors. One Wall Street joker even said: "I don't know why Joe Kennedy turned on me—I never did anything to help him."

"It's easy to make money in the market," he noted. "We'd better get in before they pass a law against it." For his new enterprises as "banker" he formed a small gang of Irish henchmen (nicknamed the "Murphia" after the Mafia) to do the menial tasks—including pimping—for him. Eddie Moore, former aide to Mayor James Michael Curley, was so near to Kennedy's heart he named his youngest son after him. Speaking of his children, Kennedy so often worked away from home, it was inevitable he'd miss the births of some of his children. He also had to call Rose periodically to get news about her and his offspring.

When the stock market crash came, he profited hugely, shorting stocks and accelerating their decline, making as much as $100 million profiting off of other peoples' disasters.

Yet, seeing the turmoil caused by the Depression, he said publicly, probably quoting a professionally prepared speech, "I would be willing to part with half of what I had if I could be sure of keeping, under law and order, the other half." Either half, of course, was a vast fortune, and Kennedy was level headed enough to realize business flourishes best when society is stable.

When prohibition came in 1920, Kennedy, the son of a one-time saloonkeeper, entered the popular and lucrative bootlegging business and began consorting with gangsters. "Elder statesman" of the mob Frank Costello even later claimed, "I helped Joe Kennedy get rich." (This is ironic, as Kennedy, in his own home, allowed only one pre-dinner cocktail—even for visitors.)

Kennedy liked to associate with the underworld, as well as gamble, and once even tried to buy a racetrack. Throughout his life, organized crime figures viewed him as one of their own. Chicago crime boss Sam Giancana once told a mistress (whom he shared with Jack Kennedy during Jack's presidency) that Joseph Kennedy was "one of the biggest crooks that ever lived." Kennedy even supplied the whiskey for his Harvard class reunion in 1922.

However, one shipment of bootleg whiskey Kennedy sent to New York was hijacked outside of Brockton by armed gangsters from Meyer Lansky's and Joseph "Doc" Stacher's Jewish gang—11 men died in the ensuing gunfight and Kennedy lost heavily.

The Charming Joe Kennedy

It was in 1924 that Kennedy made his first truly big score, not in whiskey, but in finance, when he helped fend off a takeover raid on the Yellow Cab Company. Kennedy moved into a hotel room in New York city and spent weeks of wheeling and dealing for and against Yellow Cab; the company was saved and he returned to Massachusetts a multi-millionaire—however, later Kennedy doublecrossed its owner.

Because of his shenanigans and vulgarity, Kennedy couldn't break into the Hub's highest social circles, and eventually moved from the Boston suburb of Brookline to the quaint and respectable town of Cohasset on the city's South Shore. However, even out here, the local gentry still snubbed the ever-expanding Kennedy family, and the Cohasset social club blackballed him.

Kennedy, who never permitted himself to indulge in any slavish adherent to mere facts, always claimed his exclusion from the best WASP circles was because he was Irish. That was a lie: it was because he was a shameless and indeed happily successful, crook.

Indeed, Kennedy vehemently tried to distance himself from his roots—unless of course he was trying to win sympathy as an apparent victim of anti-Irish prejudice. The third generation American once said: "I was born in America. My children were born here. What the hell do I have to do to be called an American?" Craving acceptance, Kennedy provided the beer and entertainment at Harvard class reunions until at number 25, his classmates booed him. They were only kidding, but he never went back.

"It's the snooty Back Bay bankers who are missing the boat," he said.

Eventually, in frustration, Kennedy moved his family in a private railroad car to New York, eventually planting them in the exclusive suburb of Bronxville. Later, he would use Massachusetts as the launching point for his sons' career, but that was only for political expediency and not based in any love of, or connection to, the Bay State. When later, the Irish bluebloods of New York snubbed Rose, Kennedy insisted he'd be buried back in Brookline, because at least there he knew the grounds for his exclusion.

For relaxation, he liked to sail and listen to music. Kennedy did have some taste in classical music and particularly liked the composer Ludwig von Beethoven. He once told his Irish henchmen: "You dumb bastards don't appreciate culture."

As father, he was a tyrant. He had a standing rule for his children: succeed at all costs—this would eventually result in the deaths of three of his four sons, the lobotomy of his daughter, and countless other mishaps to his grandchildren. "We want winners, " he told his family. "We don't want any losers around here."

He cruelly pushed his daughter Rosemary, who was slow (for reasons unknown), to learn faster than possible. He made the deathly-ill Jack play football. Indeed, he tried to get all his sons to get their H for Harvard sports, despite their lack of athletic ability. In public and in the media, he ensured that the Kennedys—not a particularly talented or exceptional family—were always portrayed as winners—even when they weren't.

Because of his tight control of his family and their finances, the Kennedy children were never allowed to mature-even when Jack was president, he deferred to his dictatorial father. The family rules applied to everyone—even outsiders. When Jacqueline Kennedy wanted to buy a Thunderbird, the patriarch forbade the purchase, saying, "Kennedys drive Buicks."

HOLLYWOOD, SWANSON

Ever with a roving eye for easy money and glamorous sex, Kennedy drifted to Hollywood and the fledgling movie industry budding there. He became a producer of movies that were tasteless, but profitable. His career was checkered: he plundered one movie studio, the Pathe, and helped found the giant RKO. Best yet, he got to rub elbows (and other anatomical parts) with one of the most desirable and glamorous women of her time—movie star Gloria Swanson.

The Charming Joe Kennedy

Although Swanson was married to a French nobleman (an empty title with no money behind it), with his usual directness, Kennedy began courting. He even managed to get one of his aides to take Swanson's unsuspecting husband off on a fishing trip so he could make love to the star. Eventually, Kennedy gave the marquis a job in Europe to be rid of him.

His final conquest of Swanson, perhaps the only genuine romantic love of his life, was a clumsy, incoherent mess, with Kennedy having, in the star's words, a "hasty climax."(However, at least one lover described Kennedy as being "well-endowed.")

Kennedy flaunted Swanson publicly, even bringing her home to meet Rose, who welcomed the celebrity as if she was just another of her husband's business partners. Bizarrely, the trio took a voyage round the world. Kennedy behaved openly with jealousy and concern toward Swanson, at one point, even telling a fellow passenger to stop staring at Swanson and to mind his own business. Rose generously—or foolishly— encouraged her husband for this bit of gallantry.

The financier-movie mogul showed a genuine, tender passionate side for Swanson he could not show for the cold, dispassionate Rose. He reportedly even asked the church for special permission to live with Swanson. Indeed, so intent was on he on chasing after Swanson, and so frightened was he that "the Jews would rob me blind," he didn't bother to return home in May, 1929 for his father and benefactor P.J.'s funeral.

Reportedly, not content with Rose's seemingly endless maternal exertions, Kennedy asked Swanson to have his child; she refused. Instead, they produced movies together, with Kennedy wanting to make Swanson a greater star than ever. They managed to produce some epic flops, like the aptly named disaster, "The Swamp."

When they later co-produced "Queen Kristina," Kennedy found himself in danger of losing $1million. This potential threat to his precious money made Kennedy almost hysterical. "I've never had a failure in my life," he once told Swanson between whispers; she found this puzzling.

"Queen Kristina" indeed lost money, but not for the Boston wheeler-dealer. He had structured the deal so if they made money, he and Swanson would split it equally; but if it flopped, Swanson would bear the financial burden alone. Kennedy also gave Swanson a number of gifts, using Swanson's own money (diverted through the company) to do so. When, jokingly, Swanson questioned Kennedy's honesty—understandably, a sore spot for the swindler—he abruptly left town, $5 million richer.

Swanson, on the other hand, was $1 million in the red and with an account book so snarled up from her sometime lover's financial hocus-pocus it took a year to unravel it. After three years together, Swanson had joined the long line of Kennedy's victims.

AIMING FOR THE WHITE HOUSE

The son of a string-puller and clever politician, Kennedy had a grand ambition—to be the first Catholic president. When Kennedy decided to re-enter politics, he hitched his wagon to Franklin Roosevelt's machine, brazenly buying his way into Roosevelt's camp. His (and Curley's) wheeling and dealing on Roosevelt's behalf led him to claim he won the man the nomination for president—he was not half wrong.

He made friends in the media, getting them to ghostwrite books for him and his son, Jack, and make him look good in the press. He raised his habit of incessant lying to reporters about himself and his family to an art form—now known politely as "public relations."

When Roosevelt became president, bringing the New Deal, the controversial Kennedy finagled a job working for the newly created Securities and Exchange Commission. Roosevelt, a sly comedian, must have had a twinkle in his eye when he appointed the famous stock swindler head of the finance industry's regulatory agency. However, by most accounts, the SEC was—and is—a great success.

The Charming Joe Kennedy

Kennedy decided to become ambassador to Great Britain, the most important diplomatic post available, explaining he "was intrigued by the thought of being the first Irishman to be Ambassador from the United States to the Court of St. James." Kennedy did some business favors for Roosevelt's greedy and simpleminded son Jimmy, and thus became a front runner for the job.

The foremost American president of the century met with its foremost con man, face to face, in the Oval Office to discuss the request. The polio-paralyzed Roosevelt, realizing Kennedy really believed the ambassadorship attainable, laughed so hard he nearly fell out of his wheelchair. Roosevelt then told the middle-aged millionaire to drop his pants. Literally.

Kennedy obeyed his former—and soon to be again—nemesis.

"Joe, just look at your legs," said the president. "You are just about the most bowlegged man I have ever seen. Don't you know that the Ambassador to the Court of St. James' has to go through an induction ceremony in which he wears knee britches and silk stockings...we'll be a laughingstock."

Nonetheless, Kennedy cut what appeared to be an impossible deal. He convinced Roosevelt to accept him—if he could secure permission to wear a cutaway coat and striped pants during the induction ceremony. Kennedy miraculously got his way.

When he arrived in England, initially, he played the role of diplomat well. He soon improved his considerable cussing skills by adopting the imprecations common on his new island home. The great sinner, as leading Catholic layman in America, represented his country at the coronation of Pope Pius XII; he claimed later that the pope approved of his lifestyle.

Seeing the royal couple in 1938 at Ascot, he said of the pomp and circumstance: "Well, if that's just not just like Hollywood."

37

THE AMBASSADOR STUMBLES

The movie star paradise was not to last: Kennedy had hit his peak. The trip down for him, personally and professionally, would be slow and painful. Ever the egoist, he believed that as ambassador, he could keep the United States out of war. Undoubtedly, his motives were impure: if war came, it would interfere with his lucrative Scotch importing business.

That belief was sensible—for all his faults, Kennedy was not bloodthirsty. But he took it a step—no, a jump—further: for the first time in his life, he adopted a kind of idealism: that of appeasing Hitler at all costs. He even gave a speech praising English prime minister Chamberlain's acceptance of German dictator Adolph Hitler's invasion of Czechoslovakia. The public reaction against him was huge.

After the Kristallnacht in Germany, when Nazis stormed throughout the country breaking the shop windows of Jewish merchants, Kennedy—who hated Jews, admired the Nazis, and had leanings to white supremacy—came up with an idea that was downright lunatic. He suggested the Jews emigrate to Africa.

His carefully cultivated popularity began to vanish. Privately, Kennedy loved to blast Roosevelt—not realizing there is no real secrecy in politics and Roosevelt always heard about it, and treated his maverick ambassador accordingly. Kennedy apparently was aware of the tight, private relationship between Winston Churchill and Roosevelt that was helping prop England up with arms and money and other resources, and possibly planned to blackmail the president with it. Little did he know, the British secret service, M1-5, was bugging his phone calls and spying on him....

The English public began to gossip about his philandering and stock market speculation in England. One rumor was that he exported his Scotch back home using cargo space needed for immigrants fleeing beleaguered England; another that he had profited from the invasion of Czechoslovakia. Members of Congress called for his resignation.

The Charming Joe Kennedy

Kennedy, however, held on. Believing foolishly that as ambassador, he could avoid war; he made fun of the typical "striped pants" set of the diplomatic corps. When Germany eventually invaded Norway and Winston Churchill, ready for war, replaced Chamberlain, Kennedy became a leper to the English government. Once Hitler started bombing London, Kennedy spent as much time as he could in the countryside, leaving his staff behind to brave the dangers of the Luftwaffe.

One memo from British government files stated: "Mr. Kennedy is a very foul specimen of double-crosser and defeatist. He thinks of nothing but his own pocket. I hope this war will at least see the elimination of his type." One can say that at least on the last score, the author of the memo was certainly wrong.

After Hitler invaded Poland, Kennedy left England and resigned, claiming, "Roosevelt and the kikes were taking us into war."

Both president and ex-ambassador now planned to destroy the other with insider information. They agreed to a private meeting at Roosevelt's house.

Roosevelt, possibly threatening to expose Kennedy's financial shenanigans, won the contest, but became so outraged he threw the ambassador out and told his wife, Eleanor, "I never want to see that son of a bitch again as long as I live. Take his resignation and get him out of here!"

Because of his open stance against Roosevelt—whom he referred to as a "son-of-a-bitch"— and the coming war, his career as politician was over. No matter. Roosevelt made the ambassadorship serve its purpose—it kept Kennedy out of his way and prevented the multi-millionaire from running against him or supporting a different rival.

After this and the bad press, Kennedy was finished as a political force. He had no political base to retreat to. Nevertheless, he had his—and his dream of a dynasty. He played kingmaker to his despised home state, doling out fifty grand apiece to pols he liked, it was said, and double to ones he really liked.

39

To keep the position of Massachusetts' governor open for his son, Joe, Jr., Kennedy deliberately ruined Roosevelt protege Joseph Casey, who was running for governor, by supporting Casey's opponent, Republican Henry Cabot Lodge.

As part of his scheme to ruin Casey, Kennedy got father-in-law Honey Fitzgerald to run for governor, despite his contempt for the old man. Kennedy called him a "drunken old bastard." That was being unfair—Fitzgerald was good natured and harmless by this point—although at times he laughed so hard at his own jokes that he wet his pants, even in public.

Despite their father's opposition to war, after Pearl Harbor, Kennedy's sons enlisted in the armed forces. The sickly and indolent Jack, through Kennedy's connections, landed a job in Navy intelligence, only to blunder into an affair with a woman suspected of being a spy. This woman was the anti-Semitic Inga Arvad, pretty enough for Kennedy the father himself to make a pass at her. When the FBI found out about Arvad's somewhat questionable past, the Navy fired Jack, and only by his father's intervention with the Undersecretary of the Navy was he even allowed to remain in uniform.

Kennedy, who once said he wished he had gelded his second son, then managed to arrange a job ideally suited for a playboy used to sailing: that of a PT-boat skipper. But that is another story.

Things were to go badly for Kennedy's family. He had his daughter Rosemary, who was prone to depression and considered retarded, lobotomized. One author claims Kennedy had been molesting Rosemary for some time and did this to keep her from ever spilling the beans on him, but that seems farfetched. He did, however, completely abandon her and never mentioned her name again.

The seeds of Tragedy Number One were sown in the South Pacific, when Jack's boat was cut in half by a destroyer. Kennedy made this bit of incompetence on the part of his second son, a poor PT skipper, appear a heroic act. Now an envious Joe Jr., driven by a need—stoked by his father—to be the best at everything, took off on what was to be a suicide flight mission. Joe Jr.'s final words were not for the withdrawn, indifferent mother, but rather for the pushy, controlling father.

"I'm about to go into my act," said Joe Jr. before flying off in an unreliable plane loaded with TNT, "and if I don't come back tell my dad—despite our differences—that I love him very much."

The plane the 29-year-old flew exploded in the air.

After two priests told the news to Kennedy, he told his children to be good to their mother, then locked himself alone in his room. His firstborn's death killed a part of him; the hard shell he had erected against the world cracked.

"I feel bad that I was away so much when the boy was growing up," he said, weeping. "I didn't know him like I should have. I cheated him." He later accused Roosevelt of killing his boy.

The pain deepened later when his daughter Kathleen's husband was killed in combat. "I have had brought home to me what I saw for all the mothers and fathers of the world..." he wrote.

Despite his opposition to the war, he coldly exploited whatever fame his family could get from it. He turned Jack's blunder with PT-109 into a public relations success. He also pulled strings to see the destroyer, *U.S.S. Joseph Kennedy, Jr.* commissioned, and even had his son Robert stationed to it.

THE EX-AMBASSADOR

His need to make money was undiminished, and during the war, he made as much as $100 million in real estate speculation. He bought the world's second largest building (second only to the Pentagon), the Chicago Merchandise Mart, at a rock bottom price. At the war's close, he was ready to use all his huge fortune to buy political careers for his sons—who were going into the field whether they liked it or not. He spent lavishly, pushed hard and got results.

Despite his age, he continued his sexual career—that string of shoddy conquests and glorified near rapes—with abandon.

When assaulting the mate of the future lieutenant governor of Massachusetts, he threatened her by saying: "Your husband is just a two-bit politician and I can kill his career!"

Kennedy not only competed for his sons' and daughters' girlfriends—but his sons' and their friends' girlfriends. The brothers shared their conquests with their father and vice versa. Kennedy bragged about his affairs and when doing so, as is typical, falsely inflated the number of notches on his belt.

The witty Jack frequently said to women staying with his family: "Be sure to lock the bedroom door. The Ambassador has a tendency to prowl late at night."

Kennedy—and by extension, the sons that aped him—was by nature right wing, so his friendship with Joseph McCarthy, the Hitlerian senator from Wisconsin, was a natural fit. Ironically, in 1950 Kennedy contributed $150,000 to anti-Communist Richard Nixon's senate campaign in California; Nixon nearly beat Kennedy 10 years later in a close race for president.

Kennedy landed son Robert with a choice job serving on McCarthy's fascistic investigative senate subcommittee—at first ferreting out suspected homosexuals in the state department, later hunting communists. Eventually, seeking headlines and fame for himself, he began to chase after the very gangsters who had palled around and done business with his father and helped elect his brother president.

When Jack ran for congress in 1946, filling Curley's vacated seat, Kennedy ran the campaign with his usual style, spending and lying lavishly, without any slavish adherence to any silly impediments such as ethics, honor, fairness, etc, saying he would sell his son like "soap flakes."

The war-hating Ambassador shamelessly played up his son's dubious military record. "My story about the collision is getting better all the time," said Jack, perhaps the only Kennedy who could look at his family from an outsider's point of view. "Now I've got a Jew and a Nigger in the story and with me being a Catholic, that's great."

The Charming Joe Kennedy

The Ambassador took no chances, and resorting to an old Boston election trick, even placed a janitor placed on the ballot whose name was identical with the authentic candidate running against Jack. The resulting confusion guaranteed the vote was split and delivered the victory to Jack.

The later skullduggery Kennedy employed for Jack's political career was even more brazen. It appears when Jack ran for president, Kennedy spent bribe money liberally during the primary and, through singer Frank Sinatra, pulled some underworld strings to swing West Virginia's voters, even having a sitdown with top Mafia leaders in New York face to face. Allegedly, he even used the church to launder his son's campaign funds. After Jack's election to president, Kennedy faded into the background...as the second most powerful man in the country, Jack could never stand up to this father, and Kennedy barked orders to his son over a private phone line connected to the White House.

SAME OLD JOE

Kennedy's hatred of the Fitzgeralds never abated. In 1960, right after Jack's inauguration, he threw a fancy party at the Mayflower Hotel. Seeing Fitzgerald relatives all about, he asked a secretary, "Just who are all these freeloaders?" He began to go down the guest list and asked each guest who they were.

Kennedy ran the White House through Jack. The Kennedys were bullies by nature, but denied the physical prowess to do much about it, they now took advantage of the most powerful arsenal in world history to demonstrate their manhood.

Far from being a "liberal," Jack imitated his father, who was right wing almost to the point of fascism. He once asked "how the hell any son of mine could be a goddamned liberal? Don't worry about Jack being a weak sister. He'll be tough." The Kennedy regime went from confrontation to confrontation—from the Bay of Pigs invasion—and as a result—to the Cuban Missile Crisis (the closest brush with nuclear war the world has ever seen) to Vietnam to....Suffice it to say, whenever Jack went to work, which was thankfully infrequent, it was often to conduct wars both secret and open.

The Kennedy presidency was mediocre at best, marred by lies, scandal, incompetence and belligerence, thus far. It did, however, have a very successful public relations machine in place.

But it wasn't enough to have a president as son. He forced Jack to make the young and inexperienced Bobby attorney general—an amazing slap in the face to the separation of powers in government. "Nepotism, my foot!" he yelled. "Why would anyone think that Bobby needs a job!"

Indeed Bobby was special favorite. "He's a great kid," said Kennedy. "He hates the same way I do." He also said: "When Bobby hates you, you stay hated." He tried to discourage Bobby from chasing the mob—after all, he had lots of things to hide in that department; Bobby pressed on anyway.

Another Kennedy legacy was the ingratitude and arrogance of his children, who were brainwashed from childhood into thinking nature had called them apart from mere mortals. "Never expect any appreciation from my boys," he said to Tip O'Neill. "These kids have had so much done for them by other people that they assume it's coming to them."

The old lion still had a claw or two. When his clumsy son Edward, was caught trying to get someone else to take his Spanish exam at Harvard, Kennedy squashed the issue cold and covered it up for years. Considering the Massachusetts senator's seat a special sinecure for his children, he later paid for Edward's election to it.

"I spent a lot of money for that Senate seat," Kennedy is alleged to have said. "It belongs in the family."

THE BITTER FINALE

But his end was coming. In December, 1961, Kennedy had a stroke playing golf with his niece, and hung between life and death. Jack and Bobby debated whether or not pull the plug on their father. Kennedy survived, but his right side remained paralyzed. He faced the ultimate torture: He was clear of mind, but imprisoned in a crippled body. His communication consisted of gurgling out the word "no," swearing and throwing objects at people when he was displeased. He became especially agitated when Rose was nearby.

One friend recalled seeing Kennedy reading the newspaper and suddenly crying—it had an obituary of an old friend's wife in it.

When son John had his head blown apart by an assassin, no one told Kennedy. The TV remained off, and employees claimed it was out of order. When Kennedy insisted it be plugged in, his son Ted complied, but then ripped out its cord.

His daughter Eunice later came in and said: "Jack was in an accident, Daddy. Oh Daddy, Jack's dead...but he's in heaven...Jack's okay, isn't he?" Kennedy cried again, as he had for the son that had died 20 years before.

During Jack's funeral, Kennedy remained behind in Hyannisport and watched the event on television. Widow Jackie, who had orchestrated the somewhat overdone ceremony, later brought the flag Jack's casket had been draped in to the compound. One servant, thinking it a blanket, laid it over the sleeping Kennedy. The patriarch awoke in the middle of the night, and seeing himself covered with the flag, thought he was dead and lying in state. His screams woke the entire household.

His eyes stayed wet though the winter of 1963; impotent, he lived on feebly just in time to see his son Bobby's death and the unraveling of all his work for his sons. Mercifully, Kennedy's mind began to cloud; while watching President Dwight Eisenhower's funeral, he thought it was his son Ted's.

The final tragedy, Chappaquiddick, finished him off. Ted walked in on his father and said, "Dad I'm some trouble. There's been an accident and you're going to hear all sorts of things about me from now on. Terrible things..." Kennedy held Ted's hand to his chest.

Kennedy died only in the tiniest increments. Eventually, he lost all control of his speech and later went blind. Finally, he stopped eating.... During the last moments, Eunice, Pat, Jean and Ted stood around his bed. Rose put a rosary over Kennedy's lips, letting the beads drop over his fingers. The family began to recite the Lord's prayer; before they completed it, Kennedy died.

After a long and pompous eulogy from oldtime crony Cardinal Cushing, Kennedy entered that graveyard in Brookline, where he would know the grounds for his exclusion....

THE FAMILY

His huge family, if it continues to multiply at the current rate, may very well be able to fill every political office in the nation by the year 2,097. However, without the guiding scoundrel's hand and genius around to control the Kennedy clan, that is not too likely.

With the passage of Joseph Kennedy, the family was bound to disintegrate as a political force. The children and grandchildren Kennedy are free from his control to pick their own lives. The great fortune is also rumored to be wearing down through erosion.

Indeed, the decision by Kennedy's namesake, grandson and congressman Joseph Kennedy, Robert's son, to retire from politics, may be a mark there has been a sea change in the family's vocation. They have to define their family from now on—after all, not even Joe the great negotiator and backroom manipulator could make a deal with the great killer, time.

chapter three

providence godfather raymond patriarca

New England's closest facsimile to the "Godfather" drew mixed reactions.

"If only people would realize what organized crime is, how it affects them. They don't know how powerful Raymond is. He is the most powerful man I've ever dealt with. He is a shrewd, scheming individual as well-versed in the ways of crime today as he was yesteryear. He is as ruthless in the sixties as he was in the thirties."

The speaker was Colonel Walter E. Stone, former superintendent of the Rhode Island State Police. He was testifying about Raimondo Laredo Salvatore Patriarca, then head of the United States Mafia's New England branch.

Patriarca's neighbors had a different idea about him. They recalled the baskets of groceries he sent to the poor, the money he dispensed to church and community programs, the small old-world gestures he made. Patriarca would tip his hat to ladies he passed by. The neighborhood thought of Patriarca in terms of the popular but highly glorified book and movie character, Don Vito Corleone, a man of honor and justice, who keeps order in his neighborhood. This is of course absurd— anyone whose life is spent breaking the law cannot by some odd reversal of logic be actually enforcing it.

One Patriarca worker, whose job was replenishing cigarette machines for his vending business, said while he was in the hospital for a month, Patriarca called him every day to see how he was. "They can say anything they want....but he was the best man in the world," said the worker.

Policeman Stone obviously knew that for some reason, people idealize their local thugs, viewing them in terms of Robin Hood or folk bandits. The public foolishly romanticizes the bloody, tawdry, crude crimes professional gangsters do to earn large sums of money without having to work for them.

Indeed, for some inexplicable reason, people often mark the decline of their neighborhoods in terms of the relative health of their local underworld gangs. Members of the Providence, Rhode Island, Federal Hill neighborhood, once a mostly Italian neighborhood, look back at the tenure of Raymond Patriarca as having been some sort of Golden Age in the history of their community. Thus they blatantly overlook the man's long rein of terror, which spanned decades and only ceased with death—a natural, one by the way. They forget his many murders, treachery, and other crimes.

Indeed, the image Patriarca cultivated was that of an honest businessman. Of course, no one fell for that, but people in his neighborhood did think he was polite and that he kept the thugs from the latest arrived immigrant groups—like the Hispanics—in line and, in fact, was doing the work the local police should have done.

The reality is, these kingpins—like James "Whitey" Bulger—go out of their way to appear to be friendly to the community, to shift focus from their more questionable activities—gambling, prostitution, drugs, extortion, theft—that rarely ever strengthen a community, but actually are signs of its decay and that help to undermine it. Patriarca used a coin vending machines business as his front to hide his real profession—Mafia Don.

(Even years after Patriarca's death, there still existed a certain touch of the underworld in coin vending in the Providence area, something I saw first hand. One proprietor of a pub in the Providence area had a cigarette machine. He said once when moving it from one part of the bar to another, he dropped it and coins rolled out. For that, he got a death threat by phone. "As if I'm going to take on the Mafia," he said.

Another man over the border in a small Massachusetts city had a better partnership on his coin operated games. "My partner comes by and checks to make sure the machines are doing okay," he said. "He's a businessman." He emphasized with a smile that what he said was not for print.)

Yet in many ways, Patriarca's career was not exemplary. He was convicted 18 times out of some 40 arrests—hardly a model criminal's record. Many of the crimes were lowbrow, petty nuisances—auto theft, breaking and entering, armed robbery, pimping—things usually bringing low pay and long sentences. What is remarkable is how this seedy man of limited intelligence and almost no education came to rise so high in the rigid structure of the Mafia, so that some called him the unofficial mayor of Providence and the most feared public enemy in Rhode Island.

ARRESTED DEVELOPMENT

The small, dirty, dingy industrial city of Worcester, nestled amid the low rolling hill of central Massachusetts was, in 1908, the birthplace of the future crime lord of New England. His mother, Vinceza DeNubila, was a nurse, which is somewhat, ironic, as her son would spend much of his life putting people in hospitals—or the morgue. His father Elueterio was a baker, soon to turn a peddler of liquor in Providence, where he moved his family.

The future "Padrone," or boss of New England, had an unremarkable childhood, from what is known. He attended local schools in the very Italian neighborhood of Federal Hill until the eighth grade, when he quite at age 14 to work as a jitney driver. He also became a bellboy in the ritzy Biltmore Hotel in downtown Providence. He must have seen something of the good life there, carrying bags for moneyed people, and decided he wanted to taste that world, too. The problem was, he didn't want to work at it— after only six months, he quit his studies to be a mechanic at the Providence Trade School.

It's not clear what pushed Patriarca into the criminal's life. He himself claimed that it had to do with his father's death in

1925. He later said "I lost my father and I guess I drifted a little." He claimed that his first jobs were as a salesman working out of a car, which may have been true—although he was probably retailing stolen goods.

Patriarca's first of many brushes with the law happened in May, 1926, when, aged 18, he committed some crime in Connecticut and was placed on probation. As he so often did, he violated the probation the next year. Authorities arrested and fined him $350 and doled out a 30-day suspended sentence.

Obviously the budding young felon was not much discouraged by his arrest in Connecticut, because on August 11, 1926, a policeman in Franklin, Massachusetts, nabbed him for driving on the wrong side of the road and failing to stop. Days later, police in Hopkinton, Rhode Island, investigating a hijacking gang, threw Patriarca, going under the alias "John D'Nubile," in the town jail as a suspect. He jimmied the lock and escaped—only to have the state police arrest him on August 13. A judge gave him 30 days for his trouble.

He got into the best criminal enterprise of his time—bootlegging—for which a judge fined Patriarca $100. Indeed, running liquor—and theft and armed robbery—was to be his first real entree to the criminal world. Early on, he demonstrated a treacherous streak that would serve him well in years to come. He worked as guard shipping liquor, but if bribed enough, he would let the shipment be hijacked.

His first experience of harsh time in jail came in February, 1928 when authorities caught him with a breaking and entering and larceny charge that carried a two year sentence in the state lockup. This was not a particularly promising beginning for a career criminal—he seemed to be some kind of loser—but it is a testimony both to Patriarca's resilience as well as his contempt of the law that he kept going despite these early setbacks.

LOW CRIMES AND MISDEMEANORS

He won parole in January, 1930; several months later, police arrested him again in Woonsocket as a suspicious person, but the charges were dropped. In that same month, he hatched a dangerous and foolhardy scheme to spring two convicts, "Whitey" Miller and "Pretty" McNeal, from the state jail at Howard, Rhode Island. Gunmen killed two prison workers; one of the two escapees eventually killed himself. This incident came back to haunt Patriarca years later.

It appears Patriarca almost had a need to get arrested. In September of that year, police took him in for rolling dice on a Sunday and he got a fine. Soon after, his parole was revoked and he returned to jail briefly. In November, he was paroled again, only to be arrested for violating the Mann Act, which forbids moving women across a state for "immoral" purposes. That is, he drove a woman from Providence to New Haven to pimp her. This "white slavery" Federal offense netted Patriarca a piece of a $44 kitty and a year and a day in jail. It also allowed him to see a little more of the world and expand his criminal education in the U.S. government's Atlanta Penitentiary. He got out a year later.

It isn't clear at what point Patriarca decided he was never going to go straight—some of the early daring crimes indicate a personality that was basically indifferent either to authority or punishment. In any case, it is no doubt his years in jail during his tender green years must have hardened him at least a bit and given him some valuable time to learn how to be a better criminal. Did he regret this lost time taken from his youth? He never publicly indicated it.

About a year after he left the penitentiary, he demonstrated brazen courage when he robbed the Webster National Bank at gunpoint. The police picked him up—however, for some reason, witnesses in the Worcester court recanted their testimony in court and let him go. Soon after, in Southbridge, he was charged with a robbery, but released.

PUBLIC ENEMY AT LAST

Over the next years, police in communities from Springfield, Massachusetts, to Pawtucket, Rhode Island would swoop down on Patriarca. He was arrested and discharged twice again in the space of a year, once in Providence as a suspicious person, and once in Worcester, for "lewd cohabitation." Indeed, the man who would become the image of conservative family (and Mafia Family) values appears to have been fairly promiscuous in his younger years; the Commonwealth of Massachusetts also later fined him for adultery.

So much of a nuisance had Patriarca become, in 1933, the police in Providence put him on the public enemies list; within years he topped the criminal totem as Number One. In a sense, he was making it big in his underworld. He was no longer just a minor punk—he was a recognizable menace the police could arrest anytime they caught him at night behind the wheel of a car.

"Sure I was a bad kid in Providence," he said later. "Everyone knew I was a gambler...."

And he was recognizable. He liked to look the role of a villain. Although short and slight, he liked to look tough and dressed like a movie gangster—except for his white socks—with a permanent cigar or cigarette hanging out of his mouth. He was small, but intense with a frightening temper. He had a ragged harsh mouth, which many people noted, as they did his strong, smoldering dark eyes. His appearance helped him keep his associates in line.

Speaking of his associates, it may have been as early as 1928 he was recruited to work in the local Mafia—or to sound politically correct, Italian-American social club. Just when he entered the organization is a bit fuzzy, but it appears Patriarca was first under the leadership of Frank Iacone, who was Patriarca's first "capo," or boss.

Now since the word "Mafia" has been used in so many contexts, it is almost meaningless. Iacone's gang was probably just a group of local Italian hoods who bootlegged and robbed and had some sort of ritual they used to initiate people who wanted to join them.

The real origins of the Mafia, upper case M, are hard to determine, particularly as it is supposed to be a secret society, like Sam Adams' Sons of Liberty, and most information comes from the testimony of former or imagined members. These criminals are not particularly prone to telling the truth, and they are usually bound by oath to "omerta," or silence to the authorities, so a lot of mystery remains. Often, members of a Mafia branch would just call their organization "La Cosa Nostra," which just means "This Thing of Ours." When Patriarca became Don, or head of the various Mafia branches in New England, they called his administration "The Office," because that's where he worked from.

However the Mafia at least as a concept, historically has roots that go back to Sicily, where it was a secret resistance group devoted to protecting the helpless peasants of that island from the oppression of its many invaders. So much for history. In America, it took a looser form, or forms, with members more interested in oppressing or exploiting people than in protecting them. Membership—often called being "made"— usually involves some sort of oath and a secret ritual—which is less secret now than it was since the FBI bugged Patriarca's son, Raymond Jr., when he was initiating some new members.

In any case, Patriarca senior first became a "soldier," or low level employee, in Iacone's group, or someone else's, and eventually took it over. Despite his many arrests, higher ups in the organization noticed him; he was marked for success in "organized" crime. His reputation for toughness was legendary. Certainly he had the stamina to do prison sentences, and seemed to defy the police, and risk his neck as second, if not first, nature. Life was cheap to him—at least the lives of others, if not his own, and he had the stomach to ordered the murders of uncounted people.

He romanticized the Mafia. "In this thing of ours," he once said, "your love for your mother and father is one thing; your love for 'the Family' is a different kind of thing."

53

Over the years, he would also join, then absorb another local Mafia group led by Frank "Butsy" Morelli, who worked out of Providence. By 1938, Patriarca had come under the wing of Boston mob boss and fight promoter, Phil Bruccola, who made Patriarca a capo.

Bruccola and his predecessor, Joe Lombardo, had consolidated the power of the Italian Mafia in Boston and New England, subjugating the larger and older Irish gangs. Not only did they have contacts in the more powerful and influential New York families, both Bruccola and Lombardo had a rather elegant, old world style, relying more on advice than violence. Their successor did things in the reverse.

For a while, trying to stay out of sight, he lived under the name of "Brosco" in Worcester. The police there watched him closely, and looking for information about a 1935 mail robbery in Fall River, picked up Patriarca again. They suspected him of driving a murdered Providence gangster, Andino Merola, from the Biltmore in Providence, to his death. They even forced him testify at Merola's inquest. While they had no evidence in either of the two cases, they did fine him for lying about his name.

The authorities couldn't nail Patriarca for anything worth their time over the next two years: Police in Springfield arrested him for trailing a jewelry salesman through a shopping district, but all they could charge him with was vagrancy. He also beat a charge of auto theft in Cambridge, in December, 1937.

JAIL, PARDON, JAIL

A bold thief, he worked his way up to more rewarding and dangerous crimes. On February 12, 1938 Patriarca and a colleague, Benjamin Tilley, armed with guns, held up the Wallbank Jewelry Company in Brookline, Massachusetts. To prevent any chase, the duo forced owner Clarence Wallbank, another man, and a female clerk to remove their clothes.

The two took $10,000, and what they did with it will never be known, but they didn't have much time to spend it. On February

17, police in Webster caught Patriarca hiding under a bench in the middle of a gold robbery at the United Optical Company. Unfortunately for Patriarca, when searching his car, the police found a ring with the Wallbank jewelry company's name stamped on it. It didn't take too much to figure who the robber was.

Police charged Patriarca with breaking and entering at night, carrying a revolver, possession of burglar's tools, auto theft, and conspiracy. Before his trial came up, however, on August 14, 1938 the Rhode Island state police nabbed him at the Narragansett Racetrack, no surprise, as Patriarca was a big gambler and even claimed he did it for a living. His captors took Patriarca to Boston, where he was a suspect in the robbery of the Boston-based Daniel Seidler jewelry company.

It was getting comical. Lawmen dropped the Seidler robbery charge, but had him on both Webster and Brookline robberies. Wanting to avoid a long, risky trial, he pled guilty to holding up Wallbank's, and received two concurrent three to five year sentences for that and the botched United Optical theft. Patriarca went to Charlestown jail, where Mayor James Michael Curley did his brief stretch for cheating on an exam. Patriarca's stay there was even briefer than Curley's—only 84 days, as he miraculously made parole on December 21, courtesy of the "lame duck" Governor Charles Hurley and his council.

Freed, Patriarca said he would now return to Providence to live with his "ailing mother," labor as a carpenter, and "try to make up for all this foolishness."

Excusing the crimes of his hardened felon made no sense, at least on the surface. "I guess the board just had the Christmas spirit," said one councilor. That was not true. Patriarca, one of only 10 who left jail, had greased the palm of Governor's Council member and power broker Daniel Coakley, the slimy lawyer who had got Curley off bribery charges (see Curley chapter).

The public was infuriated. Two district attorneys and three police chiefs protested. The Worcester County district attorney was dumbfounded, saying he couldn't believe "any such criminal as Patriarca could be shown clemency."

Coakley, whom ultimately the Legislature would yank off the Governor's Council and bar from holding public office, defended the decision with astonishing logic. "Everybody knew he wasn't guilty of one of them [the robberies]," he said. The Wallbank case, he claimed, had been one of mistaken identity. And the United Optical incident wasn't a robbery—after all, the police "caught him [Patriarca] before he took anything and it was a simple case of breaking and entering." True enough.

Eventually, the Massachusetts legislature looked into the pardon. A Father Fagin—who proved to be Coakley's own creation—had allegedly written glowing letters about Patriarca, seeking mercy for him. Coakley also had forged a letter from Wallbank pleading with Hurley to pardon Patriarca.

"This boy is only 28 and comes from a wonderful family, and he has a wonderful mother," gushed Coakley, who had handled the petition for pardon. "And they talk about a record! He paid a $10 fine. He committed adultery....Some idiots think that if a man is arrested, it means he's a criminal." After seeing Patriarca, he said, "I fell in love with him."

The man he had fallen in love with found himself indicted yet again in June, 1939, for armed robbery of the Oxford print shop in Brighton, a job executed two years previously. So ingrained was Patriarca's habit of lying, he even used a false address on his marriage application, when that year he married Helen Mandella, a nurse, like his mother, from Worcester.

Mandella's family was unique. Her brother was a low level state house employee under Massachusetts Governor Leverett Saltonstall's administration. Saltonstall admitted he knew of the marriage. "She is a fine girl," he said, dishing out the usual pabulum for the public while sidestepping the real issue. "and her brother is essentially a good man. There is no reason to believe the marriage will not be successful." Saltonstall, although he had grounds to do it, refused to revoke Patriarca's parole, claiming the future crime lord was "leading an exemplary life."

Seeking sunnier climes, Patriarca took off with his wife to Miami for a four-month honeymoon. He claimed he was golfing, fishing, and attending the cinema. "I don't drink and never have, so that's one bad habit I don't have to shake," he told the press. He said he was "living quietly" and that "I'm certainly living right if anyone ever did. I hope they let me alone."

He may have been telling the truth. It doesn't matter. The Miami police arrested him for giving as an address the number of a vacant lot. As every career criminal will, he claimed to the local press he was a man more sinned against than sinning.

"I served a stretch in Rhode Island when I was 19 years old, and I guess the police never forget it," he told reporters. "I didn't go out with a gun that night in Brookline and rob that jeweler, and because I know I didn't, my conscience is clear. I'll go back and face the music anytime anyone in authority in Massachusetts says I have to." He laid on it on pretty thick, saying if only the police let him alone, he would settle in Miami Beach and "live decently" in some "legitimate business."

However, back in Massachusetts, in May, 1940, a judge sentenced him to 18 months for auto theft. When he got out in September, 1941, the Massachusetts legislature was at work impeaching Coakley for his role in getting Patriarca released. Although no one proved there had been a payoff, anyone who knew of Coakley was aware altruism would have been the last motive in his thinking.

NABBED

In September, 1941, Patriarca faced two indictments for holding up the Oxford print shop when police arrested him again—his bail, drawn off a mortgaged property, was not legal. It now took a boxing promoter's (presumably Phil Bruccola's) wife to put up the money up to get him out.

When in Boston that October with his lawyer and trying to get a stay on the trial, Patriarca took a stroll outside of the courtroom. The state police were waiting for just this opportunity to arrest him. It seems a secret indictment had come down from a Worcester grand jury on the firearms and burglar's tools charge stemming from the United Optical robbery—charges he hadn't been tried on.

While Patriarca yelled for his lawyer, the police carted him off to Commonwealth Pier and the state police headquarters. Pleading guilty both to the Oxford robbery and the new United Optical charge, a judge gave him two more concurrent sentences running from two and one half to three years He went to jail late in 1941—and he wouldn't be out for three years.

After leaving Norfolk State Prison Colony on parole in May 1944, Patriarca claimed yet again he was starting a new life—now hauling fertilizer around on his brother-in-law's apple orchard in Johnston, Rhode Island.

Late in the summer, when a seasoned criminal, Walter Kelly, was arrested in Easton, Pennsylvania , he told the police about his role in the bloody 1930 failed jailbreak in Howard, Rhode Island 14 years before—the same foolhardy stunt masterminded by Patriarca. An emissary of Patriarca, said Sullivan, had recruited both him and other gunmen, one of whom was subsequently gunned down in a gang fight in New York. Patriarca, who had hid the would-be jail breakers before and after the attempt, was indicted as accessory before the fact of murder.

It appeared the Don's career was facing assassination, but the Rhode Island Supreme Court, in a much-criticized move, dismissed the indictment. After all, the statute of limitations had run out and, besides, the Providence police department's file on the prison break was missing....

MOVING UP

For the next two decades, Patriarca managed to stay out of the limelight and jail, if not the scrutiny of the law. Although, for while, it had appeared he was just another career criminal loser, things changed for him. He moved higher up in the ranks of the local Mafia from 1945 to 1949, steadily taking over "Butsy" Morelli's Rhode Island gang.

Next, Joseph Lombardo, the head of the New England mob, resigned his position to become consigliere to Phil Bruccola. In 1954, claimed the FBI, Bruccola, with the blessing of the New York Commission, gave Patriarca his throne. The shift in power was bloodless. Bruccola was low key, and decided it was better to go home to Sicily and become a chicken farmer than face the authorities, who were now turning their attention to organized crime. (The unimaginative and prosaic Bruccola lived to be over 100, dying relatively peacefully in 1987 of old age.)

Raymond Patriarca had by guts, treachery and perseverance, worked his way up the rungs and come to dominate the Mafia branches in New England. He was now a "Don," which means lord, and could run his rackets with the blessing of the Mafia bosses of New York (known as The Syndicate or The Commission). His own soldiers called him "Padrone," or boss-owner. Patriarca moved the crime capital of New England from Boston to Providence.

Getting an ever-whiter collar, Patriarca branched out into stabler, less dangerous forms of business, such as the very profitable field of bookmaking. There he assumed control of the mob wire service that relayed race results cross-country from various tracks to the booking franchises.
However, Patriarca made the price of the service so high he forced many of the old operations out of business and replaced their operators with his own henchmen.

Although he claimed to be a businessman, Patriarca did not believe in capitalism or the free market. Anyone who used other wire services had their lines torn out and their establishments trashed. One hard-headed Irishman, Carleton O'Brien, refused to stop operating his own wire service—Patriarca ordered him gunned down.

At some point, he become friends with the legendary New York mobster, Frank Costello, who became his patron in the national mob syndicate. Patriarca eventually became a very good mediator in gang disputes, a valuable tool to the national Mafia syndicate. Later, Patriarca, through Costello, also bought a piece of

the Dunes Hotel in Las Vegas, and also got a piece of Atlantic City when casino gambling was legalized there. Big surprise.
(Costello or Meyer Lansky and the Providence mob appear to have forced a partnership on John F. "Big Jack" Letendre of Woonsocket, when Letendre opened a Florida gambling operation called "Club Boheme." When Letendre refused these partners, he was gunned down outside his home in Woonsocket in 1947.)

By 1950, Senator Estes Kefauver's committee investigating organized crime named Patriarca as "king of the rackets in New England." Over the next 10 years, he got larger and stronger —becoming one of the cruelest and bloodiest crime lords in America. Unlike his predecessors, he was bloodthirsty. Patriarca was old fashioned in some ways. He tried to solve all problems by killing the people he felt were responsible for them.

Life was an unusually cheap commodity to him, and whether because of his friendship with the New York syndicate or fear of his ruthlessness or both, no one else dared tried to move into his New England territories. What Patriarca lacked in real power, he made up in reputation. Everyone, whether rightly so or not, feared him.

He also had his own Don's council made of old mobsters who had built the Mafia infrastructure—particularly the connections with corrupt law enforcement officials—he had inherited. The old men were called together during crises for advice; Patriarca also gave them a cut of the family business.

At some point, Patriarca decided he was through with the dirty work. He delegated his crimes to flunkies, insulating himself from the responsibility. To put a veneer over his real line, in the mid 1950s, he opened up the National Cigarette Service, on Atwells Avenue in the middle of Little Italy in Providence—hence the nickname of his administration, "The Office."

This gave him entrance to the lucrative coin vending industry, much favored by the mob that included pinball machines, jukeboxes, and the like. Immediately, he began to strong-arm other vendors, making them bribe him to not take away their accounts; the police began to get complaints that Patriarca machines had suddenly replaced other vendors' devices in 55 locations. So pushy was Patriarca, a judge ordered him to stop muscling in on a rival. (The family business exists to this day as, what else, Patriarca Vending.)

According to 300-pound bookmaker, smuggler of endangered birds and informer Vincent Teresa, the headquarters was like a fortress. He said, "It was impossible to move through the area without being spotted and reported." The Office was well lit and had burglar alarms; nevertheless, eventually, the FBI, as they always do, got to it.

REIGN OF TERROR

In his early years as Don in the 1950s, he kept as enforcer John "Jackie" Nazarian, one of the most feared gunmen on the East Coast. The legend goes that just mentioning Jackie's name would frighten other mobsters. When Patriarca wanted to cut one of his bookie partners, George "Tiger" Balleto, out of an operation so he could keep all the profits himself, Nazarian, in front of 22 witnesses, brazenly shot Balleto down in a restaurant.

Later to prove no one should get any good citizenship ideas and inform to the police, Nazarian strangled one of these witnesses, an ex-boxer, and left his body in a garbage dump, baling wire still around his throat. Nazarian then riddled another partner, Michael Mandella, with bullets.

Patriarca, involved with the affairs of the New York Mafia, made Nazarian an extra-big name by assigning him to kill the famous mobster Albert Anastasia of Murder, Inc. fame in barbershop in New York. The hit was a success.

Now Nazarian, flush with success, said openly, "I'm taking over the Office." Frightened he might get ground up himself by his perfect killing machine, Patriarca gave the command and Nazarian was shot down openly on the streets of Federal Hill, leaving a dice game not far from The Office.

Even if he wasn't as awesome as his reputation, he certainly knew how to look the role. With his dark hair, brown eyes—with one looking slightly up—and air of menace, he commanded respect. He usually had bodyguards with him, dressed in black coats and large felt hats.

Now he was the boss, and not the soldier. His men were obliged not only to kill on his command, they had to be careful never to give a bigger wedding gift than he did. "...if you did that, you were in a whole lot of trouble," said one associate. "You had to stick with the limits set by the bosses."

He had a hit squad always ready, getting paid large sums every week, like a retainer. Patriarca's fame grew to the point where the CIA, at the ever-scheming Kennedy brothers' request, may or may not have approached Patriarca, among other mobsters, to contract out an assassination on Cuban dictator Fidel Castro. While Patriarca later claimed the Castro accusation was crazy, it is nevertheless plausible.

Eventually, he diversified. Despite being a man both loyal to his family and mistress, he successfully backed pornographic enterprises. He also muscled into that ever popular Mafia enterprise, unions, where he engaged in offering kickback style bribes to local labor leaders to plunder union health and welfare benefits funds. Once the FBI heard him tell his crew how to deal with labor problems: "Hit them. Break legs to get things your way." If people in the union voted against his flunkies, he made sure they didn't get work.

All day long, people came into his office, and Patriarca opened his drawer for them to drop money in, after which he shut the drawer. He accepted tribute, settled disputes—sometimes between legitimate people—and kept a degree of order in his empire. Would-be mob partners proposed all sort of crimes: buying stolen bonds, opening up gambling joints for rich professionals, laying hands on special paper to counterfeit U.S. currency, and so on.

He acquired the reputation of someone who was stern, but fair—he put the patriarch in Patriarca. He claimed the worst thing a man could do was take money from someone who trusted him—and money was nothing next to principle (this may have been a moment of dyslexia). He urged his followers once to threaten a holdout "in nice but firm language," said the FBI. Should the holdout continue their recalcitrance, then "bang him in the head, but in any event, be diplomatic."

Of course, Patriarca showed a different face to the people in his neighborhood. He was personable and polite, which put people at their ease. He was open to the public, and had a charming "cat that swallowed the canary" smile, as on writer put it. Locals came in to ask him to resolve personal and small business disputes.

For instance, he patched up a quarrel between two brothers whose feud was ruining their car business. He urged his bodyguard to spend more time with his mother and send her money each week. Another time, he declined to force a divorced woman to return home to her father, a friend of his, because Patriarca felt she was a grown woman and had to make decisions for herself.

He even commanded a thief who had stolen 25 typewriters from a parochial school to return them, as "the bishop was screaming," according to the FBI.

He always denied being in the Mafia and tried to appear to stand for law and order. In reality, he was strangling legitimate businesses and sponsoring illegal, parasitical ones. In showing general contempt for the law, he steadily undermined the security of his community. He sought to appear otherwise, sending people cash at funerals, funding youth events and local churches, and always appearing willing to help the poor and needy. He apparently lived the double life without a problem. People in his neighborhood wanted to believe he would take care of them—he was certainly an immovable fixture there, and it made having to put up with him that much easier.

He grew into the role of Don, wearing cheap, conservative dark suits with only a huge diamond ring and alligator shoes for ostentation—yet he wore white socks for his bad feet. With his slicked back dark hair and eyes, his black and white shots made him look somewhat like the actor Bela Lugosi in his signature role as Dracula.

Being a boss had disadvantages. He couldn't attend weddings and funerals for fear of surveillance. Yet he became the most famous second tier crook in America. Always he claimed innocence, saying once "they never let you forget the mistakes of your youth." Of course, by "mistakes," Patriarca could only have meant the times he got caught.

Yet, for all his money, his only pleasures in the world were power and eating. He liked a good steak—"Inch, inch and a half, and they better be good," according to his butcher. He also had a busty mistress, Rita O'Toole, his private nurse (whom he eventually married). He lived in a middle class house in Providence with a large "P" on the door. For a man who spent little and lived, financially speaking, a rather average life, he certainly did a lot of money collecting. He demanded a piece of every illegal enterprise he could find in his domain.

"Where there's a buck to be made," said one associate, "he was always interested."

GROWING CONCERN

The young Gennaro (Gerry) Angiulo, a Boston bookmaker, sick of being shaken down by various Mafiosi, (Ilario Zannino, also known as Larry Baione, especially) and others, decided it was easier to pay one thief than many, and took a ride to Providence and presented the new king with an envelope with $50,000 in it, and the promise of much more from future profits. That tribute bought phone calls from Patriarca to the various Boston hoods who had tormented Angiulo, who told them, "Angiulo's with me now."

Making Angiulo a Mafioso caused some resentment in the mob's ranks—Angiulo had never killed anybody and he was something of a pushover. Nevertheless, Patriarca was willing to overlook that as long as the money kept rolling in....

Angiulo, with the lethal Zannino as his lieutenant, now became a Patriarca underboss in Boston, sending a steady stream of money 40 miles from Massachusetts' political and criminal—two intimately connected worlds—capital to Rhode Island's. This was a major enterprise: Angiulo's operation alone used some 20 offices in the Boston area. At the mob's height in the 1960s, two-thirds of all New England's murders or maimings stemmed from loan sharks collecting from their victims.

Every Tuesday and Thursday, Patriarca underboss Henry Tameleo would drive from Providence to Revere to the Ebb-Tide nightclub, and pick up the tribute destined for The Office. The Cranston, Rhode Island resident Tameleo had a key job: he handed out the orders to the capos who in turn ordered their soldiers to do the beatings and killlings. Tameleo, who had spent time as a Mafioso in New York, was nearly as famous as Patriarca himself, and held the executive power in the organization.

The Family spread out into the cleaning and dyeing, automobile, garbage collection, pharmaceutical (legal and otherwise) and real estate businesses. They owned cemeteries (a good investment given Patriarca's homicidal tendencies), a North Shore country club, dude ranches, and a New Hampshire ski resort. They had 50 "made" members all over New England. No other Mafia Don challenged his authority in his empire—which, at its height, ran from Portland down to Hartford, and included Boston, some of Worcester, and of course, Providence and its environs. Springfield and Worcester were co-shared with New York dons.

Patriarca shunned publicity and scowled at reporters and photographers—although his vanity made him read everything written about him. He only gave orders over the phone now. However, while police may not have been able to nail the wiser, more cautious Patriarca on anything indictable, they were certainly aware of what he was up to.

In 1955, a terrified addictive gambler from Providence decided that the government was less frightening than Patriarca and held up a bank in Boston for $4,470. When arrested, he said he owed the Don $1,500. "I was told by a member of the Patriarca mob that I had until Thursday to get the money, or else," said the gambler. "Patriarca is the mayor of Providence."

(The organization took odd steps to collect money; the fat and buffoonish informer Teresa once put a victim's hand in a piranha tank to force him to pay what he owed.)

In 1957, the Massachusetts Crime Commission noted he was the most powerful man in the $2 billion a year underground gambling industry in the Bay State. The police received many tips—anonymously, of course—about Patriarca's secret empire.

Patriarca may have become more white collar, doing drug distribution, loansharking, gambling and other "cleaner "forms of crime, but the lethal temper was still in place. When at the Rockingham Park Racetrack in Salem, New Hampshire, he happened to see fellow Mafioso Joe Valachi, the famous "rat" who in the early 1960s opened the country's eyes to the prevalence of organized crime.

Valachi told Patriarca that a horse named Hi Bobby was "made," or drugged, and would win the race. Patriarca bet $5,000 on the horse. Well, there is no honor among thieves, and Hi Bobby came in fifth.

"So that horse was made!" yelled Patriarca at Valachi. "If you come near me again, I'll kill you!"

Indeed, he took a dim view of human nature. "I'm a man from Missouri," he once said, "and I don't trust anyone. I don't trust my left hand with my right hand."

He may not have been the ideal boss, either. Once he put up $22,000 for his men to pick up some stolen cigarettes. The FBI got to the cigarettes first. Instead of writing off his losses, Patriarca demanded his crew pay him back the seed money!

Another time, Patriarca ordered one of the white-haired councilors of his family, to kill his son, who was swindling an Office-backed business. "I can no killa my kid," he complained. "They insist ona it...they say I gotta killa my kid....I knowa I losa face, but I can'ta help it."

The old man told Patriarca face-to-face he demanded respect.

"Respect? You demand what respect? Don't you come in this joint giving me respect when your kid robbed my eyes out blind. I don't want to hear none of that shit. How much respect did you show us when you couldn't whack out that kid of yours?"

Weeping, the old soldier claimed he couldn't do it. Patriarca all but exiled the soldier from the family; it took the intercession of underboss Tameleo, (nick-named "The Referee") the boss' right hand man, to even allow the old man to remain in the family.

None other than Bobby Kennedy, the son of bootlegger and honorary Mafioso Joe Kennedy, cross-examined Patriarca during a Senate Rackets Committee hearing in May, 1959. So cocky was Patriarca, he was the only one of six witnesses not to cite his Fifth Amendment rights. He discussed the coin vending industry, among other things. The meeting was tense, to say the least, and the abrasive Kennedy lit so harshly into Patriarca that the Don's external shell cracked a bit and he threatened not to speak anymore. (Later Kennedy would try to employ the Don to kill Castro in the ill-fated "Operation Mongoose.")

Patriarca claimed that he had had various jobs, working as a restaurant "counterman and manager, like," for a while. Then, he said from 1944 until 1950, he made a living playing horses. Finally, with $80,000 his mother had left in him the cellar of her house, he finally bought into a coin operated machines business. He kept changing the particulars of this story, demonstrating he was a rather imaginative, if not entirely consistent, liar. Kennedy kept probing, until Patriarca threatened to plead the Fifth, which he said didn't want to do.

"I've been trying to get this off my chest for 20 years!" he said. " One thing about me, I've always been a man of my word and I'll die that way. There isn't an [coin] operator in Providence who would say a bad word about me."

At least not on the record.

MAKING THE BIG LEAGUES

Patriarca, in Stalinist fashion, had so ruthlessly mowed down his competitors that the national syndicate decided the man was first rate corporate material. Noting his resolve and speed, they gave him a slot on their national board of directors, founded in the 1930s, representing the Mafia of New England.

He had a high standing among his national peers, a combination of statesmanlike sagacity and viciousness. Patriarca's status in the national Mafia had nothing to do with his real power, which was relatively small compared with the larger, higher profile families from New York and other places. Although far from bright—at age 22 he had the I.Q. of a 12 year old—the Providence Don's interpersonal skills, to use a current piece of corporate jargon, were much valued in resolving disputes between these families and those from other larger organizations beyond.

He also leant out his assassins to other Dons, like Carlos Marcello of New Orleans. As mentioned above, he sent Jackie Nazarian to shoot the famous founder of Murder, Incorporated, Albert Anastasia. He also unsuccessfully tried to prop up Joseph Colombo, the head of the Profaci family in South Brooklyn, gunned down in 1971.

But Patriarca also took orders from the Commission. When New York Don Joseph Bonnano held a small revolt against the syndicate, Patriarca obeyed the Commission's ruling that "no one was to do any business with Bonnano's group." When Bonnano was exiled for his defiance, Patriarca said it was Bonnano's own fault and was caused by his greed.

He needed permission from the Commission to make soldiers—he couldn't do it on his own. The Commission wouldn't recognize anyone he made on his own. By the 1960s, the Commission feared the FBI would infiltrate their ranks, and forbade Patriarca to open the books and officially make more Mafia soldiers. So Patriarca relied more and more on "associates" to do his dirty work. He employed members of the Irish gangs of Boston, like the Winter Hill Mob, but that was on a freelance basis. He called these recruits his "suckers," and treated them with contempt. His bad handling of his own crew and associates was to prove his downfall in the years to come.

In the early 1960s, he and New York Don Tommy Luccese invested as a silent partners in the doomed Berkshire Downs racetrack in Hancock, Massachusetts, using as a front man the great mob fraternizer and go-between, the late Frank Sinatra—and Sinatra's friend, Dean Martin. When the relationship became public, Sinatra, as usual, huffed and puffed and said he resented the allegation, claiming to a senate committee it was all "hearsay." For his part, Patriarca said he had never "met the gentleman in my life."

However, so involved was Patriarca with the doomed track he even had his own state senator on the payroll to sponsor legislation to help him get favorable racing dates.

Hating his bad publicity, in September of 1961 he proved money talks and took out an ad in the *Providence Journal Bulletin* to complain about his bad treatment in its pages.

"Since my release from prison in 1944 after completion of a sentence for a crime committed in 1938 when I was 30 years of age, my time has been continuously and assiduously employed in honest endeavors." He said his years in prison had made him decide to go straight. "This resolution has been conscientiously and strictly maintained. I challenge you to prove by competent evidence that I have since, in any degree, deviated from that resolution by my engagement in any illegal or criminal enterprise or activity."

Of course, he brought his family into it. "The tranquillity of my family has many times and oft [ignore the redundancy] been disturbed by the rehashing of my criminal record in your news columns. I, more than you, deplore that record. How bitterly do I realize the truth of a great poet's words 'The evil that men do lives after them; the good is often interred with their bones.' Your newspapers seem to take a fiendish delight in their unwarranted and unjustifiable [ignore the redundancy] characterizations of me which slyly infer that I am now and have always been engaged in illegal activities."

He wondered what he could expect from a newspaper "which has often paraded in its obituary columns the peccadilloes of many former decent Rhode Island citizens." Without meaning to, Patriarca said more about himself in that ad than he was ever forced to do under oath. He even quoted Shakespeare. "The evil that men do lives after them; the good is oft interred with their bones."

When Patriarca died, there was not much good to inter.

BIG BROTHER WAS WATCHING

Little did Patriarca know it at the time, but he was the biggest informant in his own family. In 1962, the FBI had invaded the sacred throne room in National Cigarette and planted an eavesdropping device there right in his office. Over the next three years, they listened in. He revealed to the federal government not just his own operations, but those of the national La Cosa Nostra, as well. When the bugging became known, his reputation was tarnished, even if the evidence gathered was inadmissible in court.

The buggings allowed the FBI to tip off two victims, Willie Marfeo and John Biele, of Patriarca's desire to kill them. After the bugging stopped, Patriarca was able to get his way and got them both.

The picture the bugging transcripts painted of the CEO of New England crime was interesting. Things were good for the House of Patriarca. The Don had solid police and political connections. The Family had "in the bag" a police chief, a state official, two licensing officials, a court administrator, and assorted state senators and representatives. He kept a bank account called "Raymond's Escrow Fund" in place to payoff legislators—after—and only after—they had delivered the goods. He refused to pay out $25,000 from it to the legislature when his request for an extended racing season for his track failed.

The authorities also overheard discussions about secret ownerships of legitimate businesses, the hijacking of 20,000 cases of shoe polish from Chicago, bookmaking, fencing, and so on. The tapes revealed the two faces of Patriarca—at one moment, he's telling a distraught father he will make sure his errant son visits his sick mother and sends her money; the next, he's giving orders to break legs.

Patriarca told a Rhode Island businessman to forget a $17,000 contribution made to a politician high up in the Rhode Island government who was defeated for reelection. He got good treatment for his soldiers by the parole board, and even worked with another shady governor's councilor, Patrick "Sonny" McDonough, to get Zannino sprung from jail.

The tapes show Patriarca telling an associate to "contact his friend who is allegedly extremely close to Attorney General Edward W. Brooke of Massachusetts and have him arrange to release the $100,000 bond that is being held by the Massachusetts Court" for civil suits.

Patriarca even complained on tape that he couldn't get Massachusetts Lieutenant Governor Francis Belloti to accept $100,000 in mob money for his election campaign for governor in 1964. Not that it mattered—Patriarca had spread the rumor around Belloti had accepted the money, anyway, and ruined Belloti's bid.

In July 1962, a high up state police official informed Boston underboss Angiulo they were going to raid the gambling joints on Revere Beach. The five Patriarca books were shut down; the independents were nailed. A week later, the five Patriarca establishments reopened for business.

However, the relatively quiet lull in gangland that had prevailed in the 1950s changed in the next decade when two Boston Irish gangs, the Winter Hill mob in Somerville, led by "Buddy" McLean, and the McLaughlin gang of Charlestown, went to war over one hoodlum's drunken unwanted pass at a girl. (Word has it that the thug whose girlfriend's charms George McLaughlin found so irresistible, Andy Petricone, fled Boston for fear of his life. He became an actor—landing a role in the movie "The Godfather.") Before the war ended, some 50 men would die.

So violent did things get for mob operations, Patriarca said, "If the killings don't stop, I'll declare martial law." He told his men he would sit George McLaughlin down in a chair and "tell him to forget this beef and stop the war. If he says no, then you can kill him right in that chair."

He actually did try to broker an agreement between the two factions in 1964, but the McLaughlins showed up armed. Frustrated, The Referee Tameleo said, "Go kill each other."

The peace attempt failed, Patriarca, sick of the money it was costing his operation, took the side of the Winter Hill gang and helped destroy the McLaughlins to bring about peace—and of course, fill the places of the slain with his own henchmen. He personally had to order the deaths of a dozen men.

One of these victims was a stickup man named Edward Deegan, who robbed Angiulo's bookmakers. Joe "The Animal" Barboza killed him, but later fingered Tameleo, sending the old man to jail for the rest of life and nearly getting him the death sentence. Before he was arrested himself, however, Barboza killed the murderer of Buddy McLean, Steve Hughes, and then his brother, Connie Hughes, the McLaughlins' two most dangerous men.

And Patriarca also had to keep the arrogant Angiulo in line. Several times he listened to high level Mafiosi complaining about Angiulo's rudeness. At one point, Angiulo, thinking he was being cheated, so badly insulted some mobster brothers from Worcester the brother petitioned Patriarca for the right to kill Angiulo. Patriarca promised the brothers if it happened again, he would let them kill Angiulo with his blessing, and forced the Boston bookmaker to apologize.

Another strike against Patriarca came in 1963. The imprisoned bad tipster Joe Valachi, expecting to be murdered by his former boss, New York crime lord Vito Genovese, picked up a pipe and crushed the skull of the Genovese soldier he thought was out to kill him. The publicity he triggered after this move changed the way the world looked at organized crime. Cross-examined, he named Raymond L.S. Patriarca the head of the New England Mafia—not a big surprise to the people of Providence. The Don sued the *Boston Herald Traveler* for libel for printing the accusation.

Transcripts from the bugged office show Patriarca saying that if he was questioned about being a member of the mob he would say the only Mafia he ever heard of is the "Irish Mafia the Kennedys are in charge of." He planned to deny he had even heard of La Cosa Nostra until Valachi had brought it up.

In 1963, Colonel Stone, appearing before the Senate, set the record straight about Patriarca the crook, as well. He painted a portrait of a strong-arming dictator ruling an empire of fear by violence and murder—the Don also avoided doing the crimes himself; he told others to do it for him.

"Patriarca is in the background," said Stone.

Incensed, Patriarca issued a press statement, getting things reversed, saying the senate hearings smacked of Nazi Germany or Communist Russia when it was his actions that were reminiscent of a fascist state. "If I am responsible for all the crime in Rhode Island, why hasn't Colonel Stone presented some evidence against me to a Rhode Island grand jury or, if I have violated federal law, evidence to a federal grand jury?"

He said, "A person would have to be very credulous to believe that a small group of Italians are the overlords of all crime in the United States. (It is worth noting here that Patriarca didn't think violating state statutes were crimes—only federal ones. He was a centralized thinker to the last.)

He responded to Stone's charge of "past-posting," or accepting bets on races that had already been won. "His charge that I have been engaged in the dishonest practice of placing wagers on horses after the winners have been determined is a product of a fantastic mind," he said. "Evidently I have a higher opinion of the state and local police forces' ability than he has....I never doublecrossed anyone....I am engaged in a few legitimate private enterprises." (According to the FBI, that final sentence was the only accurate thing he said, if you emphasize the adverb "few.")

When that fall, authorities summoned him to court in Providence to testify before a grand jury, the wily Don avoided the waiting press by arriving in a Volkswagen and coming in the back entrance. Patriarca complained to the prosecutor that his wife had cancer, his son had dropped out of college, and he didn't need anyone dragging his name in the mud. His tactics worked: the grand jury report stated it didn't believe there was any organized crime in Rhode Island

UNEASY LIES THE HEAD THAT WEARS THE CROWN

In 1965, his wife Helen died, leaving him a son, Raymond Junior—a man who had a Samuel Adams-like ability to destroy family owned businesses. The two Patriarca men shared the same name, and that was about it. Patriarca's desire to create an underworld dynasty destroyed everything—his son was a weak bungler, a joke in the underworld. Junior, as he was called, aroused his father's wrath when he invested in the Bonnie & Klyde Delicatessen, flaunting the crime connection publicly, a grave taboo (the sandwiches were reported to be delicious, however.). Eventually, Junior would almost immediately ruin the business the father had spent half a lifetime building up.

With his wife's death, Patriarca also took up openly with his busty mistress, Rita O'Toole, a hostess at a lounge.

In that same year, a drug addict named Raymond F. "Baby" Curcio with a habit bigger than his IQ burglarized the house of Patriarca's brother, Joseph. At this point, it would have been unwise to grant Curcio a life insurance policy. In February, Patriarca summoned a hit man, Nicholas Palmigiano, and said he wanted Curcio "nailed" and wanted it done "right away" and dictated where it should be done. The killers lured Curcio into range with the promise of a lucrative housebreak, and on the car ride to the mythical job put about five bullets into the unsuspecting drug addict's head.

Upon visiting Patriarca's office the next morning, Palmigiano found the boss smiling. Patriarca told him he had done a "good job" and told him to become scarce because "there will be a lot of heat up here." That was not the last of the assassin, however...Like some of the murders Patriarca ordered, this one would come back to haunt him.

His "floating," or mobile dice games, were Patriarca's special pride and joy, and to hold them up was a quick way to earn one way trip to the grave, as three hoodlums learned. In the summer of 1966, with Patriarca's blessing, his henchmen killed Rocco DiSiglio, a small time hoodlum who had been tipping stickup men to where they could hit Mafia dice games. The murder order came from Angiulo, who told one of DiSiglio's fellow robbers to do it or be killed himself. However, Angiulo could make no hits without getting permission from Tameleo and Patriarca.

One account has the murderers, while on a beach in South Boston, telling DiSiglio to "drink the ocean," and put several bullets in his head. They took the corpse and put it in DiSiglio's new sports car for someone to find in Topsfield, Massachusetts.

DiSiglio was just one of the little people Patriarca was constantly decimating. Being a Mafia chieftain had its drawbacks—he had to spend a great deal of time plugging little leaks in his empire, and the body count may have run into the hundreds.

Later that summer, another tough but small time crook, Willie Marfeo of Providence, also became one of Patriarca's victims. Marfeo ran a dice game in a Federal Hill tenement. Although he was probably not guilty of it, he was a suspect in the 1962 murder of Patriarca enforcer "Jackie" Nazarian, who himself was a suspect in the 1955 slaying Mafia associate, "Tiger" Balleto...The eye will discern a pattern here....

In any case, Marfeo's operation sucked away customers from the regular rackets and made the police more interested in Federal Hill than Patriarca liked. Police told Patriarca Marfeo's game would make things "red hot."

Tameleo, Patriarca's underboss, visited Marfeo, and told Marfeo to end the small, low profit game. Marfeo slapped Tameleo and said, "Go tell Raymond to go shit in his hat."

"You're a dead man," said Tameleo.

When Patriarca heard of his underboss' treatment, he nearly cried with fury. "Why didn't you shoot him right then?" he asked.

"I didn't have a gun," said Tameleo.

Marfeo kept his game going and would-be killers made several attempts on his life. In the summer of 1965, Barboza, the sadistic mob hitman from New Bedford, Massachusetts, was called in and given the contract. Patriarca said: "I want him wiped out. I want it done right away." Barboza, wanting to ingratiate himself with the Don, offered to kill Marfeo gratis, as it "would open a lot of doors."

(Barboza was one of about 75 freelancers Patriarca used for odd jobs. He also liked having them around because he knew they would keep his own soldiers in line. Barboza had a strange relationship with Patriarca; he hoped, foolishly, to be the first non Italian made by the Mafia. When met the Don, he noted the boss' lizard-like lips, which were purple because of his diabetes. He also noted the "Office" was a seedy place. He said little when they first met, struck by Patriarca's expensive ring. Later he explained his silence by saying, "I was thinking how I could bite his finger off and get that diamond ring.")

Underboss Tameleo showed Barboza a photo of Marfeo, along with his hangouts. However, when Barboza was picked up on unrelated charges, he was unable to fulfill the contract and the assassination was postponed.

On the morning of July 13, 1966, a short, stocky man in a straw hat and white shirt walked into the Korner Kitchen restaurant, tapped Marfeo on the shoulder and pointing a gun at him, forced him into a telephone booth. When inside, the man shot Marfeo four times and calmly walked out.

A year later, his status among his peers and workers plummeted. During the income tax trial for one of his associates, Louis " The Fox" Taglianetti, (who of course was later murdered), the FBI revealed they had bugged the Atwells Avenue office.

Shaken, with the entire underworld secretly laughing at him, he moved his operation across the street to his Nu-Brite

Cleaners office and never returned. In 1967, the *Providence Journal* published excerpts from the transcripts, making Patriarca simultaneously the most public and the most private man in Rhode Island. So incensed was Patriarca, it was reported he temporarily put a contract out on his own brother, Joseph, head of security, for allowing the bug to be planted in the first place!

"You dumb son-of-a-bitch," he screamed at Joseph. "I oughta hit you in the head for this. For Crissakes, we could all go to jail."
(Interestingly, the bugs revealed Patriarca complaining to his closest and most trusted associates—to the degree he trusted anyone—that he was being libeled by the press and that Colonel stone was almost 100% wrong about him.)

Now Patriarca became obsessed with bugs and informants, and even bought an electric scrambler box that emitted noises to cover everything he said. If the box made it impossible for electronic eavesdroppers, it also nearly did the same thing for those trying to listen to what he had to say. He ordered everyone not use their home or office phones. He had a bug sweeper go through his office regularly, and built a device proof apartment more like a fortress than a home over the Nu-Brite address on Atwells Avenue.

Rudolph Marfeo, brother to Willie, had sworn revenge, and was now a thorn in his side and needed to be eliminated. "I don't want to hear any more stories," said Patriarca to hit man Red Kelley. "I just want him killed."

THE ANIMAL ATTACKS

After Barboza had helped wipe out a number of the holdouts in the Winter Hill-McLaughlin war, it was his turn to go. While on a Mafia errand, police, possibly acting on an Office tip, arrested Barboza, who had an M-1 rifle in his car. His bail was set at $100,000. While sitting in jail, he hoped the Office would pull some strings and help him.

Patriarca had other ideas. "Barboza is a [fucking] bum," he said. "He's expendable." Patriarca had even told Marfeo's brothers

Patriarca had other ideas. "Barboza is a [fucking] bum," he said. "He's expendable." Patriarca had even told Marfeo's brothers that Barboza had killed Marfeo, but before they could get to Barboza, however, Barboza was under arrest.
When in a North End club trying to extort money to post bail for their boss, Patriarca gunmen shot down two of Barbara's crew. The bodies were placed in South Boston to make it look as their murders were part of the war. However, an informer turned the Patriarca gunmen in and Ralphie Chong, a Patriarca soldier, was arrested as an accessory and given a harsh sentence. The rest of Barboza's crew was gunned down or arrested; as he sat in jail, the Animal's saw his dreams of greatness ruined.

The message was clear for Barboza. "I never thought the blood oath did anybody any good if Raymond decided they were too hot for his health," he noted. Patriarca, he decided, was an "old fool" and a "cold-blooded bastard."

So the sucker and Mafia wannabe threatened to kill Angiulo and Larry Zannino. He told his friend Chico (Joseph Amico) to kill one of Zannino's strong arm men; Amico himself met assassination. At this point, the rage in Barboza boiled over and he even called the Padrone himself a "fag."

This insult to his manhood led Patriarca to command an all out assassination attempt be made on Barboza the minute he left jail. "That dirty nigger bastard," said Patriarca, "I'll kill him. He's gonna get killed in or out of the can. You send the word to him—and that's all there is to it."

The DA, learning of this, made sure Barboza never got out. Realizing he couldn't get at Patriarca with a gun, Barboza, also called "Baron," decided he'd use his testimony. The Animal now turned Angiulo in for the DeSiglio murder and Patriarca in for the Marfeo one; indictments came down. That day, reportedly, two of Marfeo's brothers tried to kill Patriarca during a wild racing car gun battle through the streets of Providence. Patriarca's standing in the commission was compromised and there was speculation the old man might be deleted from the roster himself for fear at his age, he might turn. His men suggested he hide in Haiti. Barboza

Angiulo beat the DeSiglio rap, and while Patriarca's men (Steve "The Rifleman" Flemmi and Frank "Cadillac "Salemme; see the Bulger chapter) may have tried to blow up Barboza's lawyer's car, they failed to kill the attorney. During the trial, Barboza taunted Patriarca, who called him a rat. Barboza urged the Don to violate his mother's corpse.

In March 1968, a jury found Patriarca guilty in the Marfeo killing and he got five years and a $10,000 fine. It was one of the biggest blows to the Patriarca corporation. (However, in 1976, the mob got Barboza, gunning him down in San Francisco). In April, 1968 one month later, Patriarca's thugs, wearing masks, shotgunned Rudolph Marfeo and a friend, Anthony Melei in Pannone's Market on Pocasset Avenue.

Certainly it all must have seemed tedious and joyless for the aging Don, whom some think might have wanted to get out of the rackets at this point. Certainly, he was showing his age. While at a press conference, an associate noticed a few threads on his jacket. "I'm an old man," was the reply of the jackal in winter. "I don't care how I look."

Finally after exhausting all his appeals, in 1969, Patriarca started serving his sentence for killing Willie Marfeo in the Rhode Island state prison, but was moved to Atlanta to finish the sentence—that way, it was hoped, his power would be cut. Reportedly he got no special privileges in maximum security and worked a janitorial job seven days a week—for which he got a commendation from the officials.

Yet like the famed New York don, Vito Genovese, he was frightening even while doing time. Patriarca's son Junior visited him in Atlanta, and relayed orders back to the crew waiting back at The Office. In 1969, he was indicted again, with six others, for conspiring to murder Rudolph Marfeo, Willie's brother. Patriarca swore to the presiding judge his innocence "on my dead wife and children."

Patriarca enlisted a priest to perjure himself and say he had been with Patriarca the day Marfeo and Melei were murdered. Assistant Attorney General Vincent Cianci, now mayor of

Providence, proved that the priest that day had been at a baptism in Maryland. The priest recanted, and in March, 1970 Patriarca got another 10 year sentence.

Patriarca ordered yet another mobster's death, this time Robert Candos of North Attleboro, a 30 year old bank robber, because of rumors that the hoodlum was about to testify against him. Candos' skeleton was found in North Attleborough 22 months after the slaying.

In 1972 US. Select Committee on Crime questioned Patriarca about *The Godfather*. "There was a lot of fiction in it," he said. "People like to read that stuff. You could come out with *The Patriarca Papers* tomorrow and make a million dollars on it."

In a jail interview, he said organized crime was a "myth" created by prosecutors and policemen looking to get bigger budgets for their agencies. (He didn't explain where the many bodies that kept cropping up in his world originated.) He claimed his incarceration away from Rhode Island was "harassment." He said he never missed a day's work as janitor, spent time writing letters to his family and reading books—nonfiction, with lots of American history.

All this in between running his crime empire remotely.

"How many more Watergate-style revelations do we, as Americans, need to convince us that the Government is quite capable of 'manufacturing' or 'losing' evidence?" Patriarca wrote.

He fought hard to get out, enlisting the aid of many strange helpers to work on his behalf. The future Chief Justice of Rhode Island Joseph Bevilacqua, along with other public figures, darkened his career by his entanglement with the Don when he wrote a letter on Patriarca's behalf. In it, he said the Boss was "a person of integrity, and, in my opinion, good moral character."

A monsignor wrote of Patriarca: "He was kind and charitable to the needy and aged. Many times, although they suspected it, the recipients of his charity did not know he was their donor." The same churchman said the Don was a "stabilizing influence" among the young. This speaks for itself. Yet another man, a black attorney and former prosecutor, also was won over to Patriarca's cause.

BACK ON THE STREET BUT STILL IN JAIL

After six years as a prisoner, Patriarca left the Adult Correctional Institution in Rhode Island in 1975, returning to his office at Coin-o-Matic (where the sole decorations were a photos of a prizefighter and a race horse). Right away, there were four gangland killlings around Providence—as well as a wedding: Patriarca his long term mistress, Rita O'Toole.

His very early parole (only half his sentence served) which had influence peddling written all over it, caused a lot of publicity and controversy. "It happens every couple of years about this time," said Patriarca. "It's politics, but I'm used to it."

He felt persecuted, and even told a newspaper columnist he objected to what had been written about him and was ready to complain to his parole officer he was being harassed by the *Providence Journal*. "You had to put a nail in the coffin by putting words in some old guy's mouth that I only killed my enemies," Patriarca said to the columnist. "You had the old lady saying I was always polite, always tipping my hat. I know what you were doing,. You had to put in all that Godfather stuff, didn't you?"

He was now 68, sickly, badly diabetic, with a bad heart, and more paranoid than before—he claimed police cars drove by him all the time watching what he was up to. "No, I never go out anymore," he said, "because people are always coming up to me when I do." Of his office, he said, "This place is as bad as a jail. I might as well be in jail."

Feeling he hadn't received enough tribute while in jail, on August 14, 1975, he set an example to his ragtag empire of hit men, hijackers, loansharks and other assorted scum. That day, he staged a robbery of about $3 million in cash and jewelry at the Bonded Vault company—it was the second biggest heist of that sort ever done, and most of the money came from Patriarca's own Mafia employees.

Bonded Vault company—it was the second biggest heist of that sort ever done, and most of the money came from Patriarca's own Mafia employees.

The leader of the robbery, a lifelong felon named Robert J. Dussault, was living it up with a hooker when he heard the Providence gang wanted him dead. Somehow, when a three man hit squad caught up with him in Las Vegas, he talked or bribed his way out of it and went on the lam, eventually getting caught for a crime he hadn't committed. He "flipped," and entered the Federal witness protection program. Once again, Patriarca's mistreatment of the help worked to undo him.

In 1980, he moved to Johnston, out of the city, out of the hub. Ironically, that same year, he and the FBI together won the fight to bar the publication of the tapes made from the bug in his office in the 1960s."Justice always comes through," said Patriarca.

It was a hollow victory. His diabetes resulted in a gangrene infection in his toe, which the doctors amputated. The law, his own diseases and past would now conspire together to whittle him away until there was nothing left.

Every day he commuted to his National Cigarette and Coin-a-Matic offices to hold court amidst vending machines. In sunny weather, he'd stand outside on the sidewalk, talking to or scowling at passers-by and cursing the FBI, the press, and Bobby Kennedy. He become, in effect, like King Lear in the moors.

Yet in this time he expanded—over the next years, he got his New Haven underboss, the vicious William Grasso, to take all of Connecticut for the House of Patriarca's exclusive use. Grasso became, in effect, the new underboss, holding more power than Junior and eventually putting him under his thumb.

THE BITTER END

The authorities now made the last few years of his life miserable, piling indictment on top of indictment. Although arrested and charged again and again, he was able to plea bad about the possibility of kidnapping Junior Patriarca. Thus, Palmigiano earned himself a death sentence. When a boss told one of Palmigiano's friend to kill Palmigiano, he refused, and was tortured and murdered himself. The police picked Palmigiano up carrying a gun illegally, and he spilled the truth about his murder of drug addict Curcio. Patriarca was again indicted....

On December 4, 1980, the over-eager state police scooped Patriarca a day ahead of a pre-arranged public arrest planned to be done jointly the Providence police. This almost ignited a feud between the two law enforcement agencies. While in court, Patriarca, like all graying mobsters in court, claimed he was having chest pains. At Miriam Hospital, his round-the-clock guard at the hospital cost the state $800 a day.

When arraigned at his hospital bed, Patriarca, suffering from unstable angina, hardening of the arteries and severe depression, began to weep. His lawyers claimed the ailing crime czar's death was certain if he didn't get bail. Patriarca himself feared his diabetes would force surgeons to start to "cut higher and higher." Of course, Patriarca had never shown such pity to any of his victims....

Yet another murder bobbed to the surface when in March, 1981 he was indicted by a Bristol County, Massachusetts grand jury for Candos' slaying. He arrived in court on a stretcher with medical personnel attending him: Things looked dismal for the CEO of the New England underworld....

In June, Rudolph "Rudy" Sciarra one of his top men, got life for delivering the guns used in Curcio murder. However, Patriarca's trial was postponed because of his ill health, with cardiologists from Boston and Rhode Island claiming Patriarca would die from the stress. But the reality was, Patriarca was about to die anyway, and at the least they could have saved the state some expense by hastening it.

Law enforcement agencies kept fighting over Patriarca's soon to be corpse. That September, he was again before yet another judge, this time for labor racketeering in Miami with

Law enforcement agencies kept fighting over Patriarca's soon to be corpse. That September, he was again before yet another judge, this time for labor racketeering in Miami with Arthur Coia, the secretary treasurer of the Laborers International Union of North America.

"I was a bootlegger," he said to the judge. "I was a gambler. But since I got out of prison in 1945, I've done nothing wrong."

Come March 14, 1984, the authorities virtually hounded him all the way to his near deathbed, when a judge ruled had to stand trial for the racketeering case; the ruling was reversed. It didn't matter. Patriarca was clearly slipping, and his employees prepared for promotions in the new regime....

One doctor described Patriarca as a "wasted, psychologically depressed tearful elderly man." His last impotent, unhappy days are reminiscent of those of the other great stringpuller, Joe Kennedy's: both men had lived long enough to become caricatures of themselves. Patriarca was now in a haze, and always had someone following his car to make sure he didn't do anything dangerous.

On July 11, 1984, a North Providence rescue crew arrived at an apartment on Douglas Avenue to find the 76 year old Patriarca in a woman friend's apartment—he was without a pulse or respiration or blood pressure. They brought him to Rhode Island hospital, where he died—apparently of a heart attack.

When underboss Gerry Angiulo, sitting in court in Boston, got the news, he hung his head sadly. Later, while staring down Jeremiah O'Sullivan, the lawyer heading the special Justice Department Organized Crime Strike Force in New England, Angiulo muttered something in Italian, possibly a curse. Later, he said, "They killed him."—meaning the Justice Department. In 1986, Angiulo himself was sentenced to 46 years.

Patriarca's death was a big event, making the front pages of the newspapers and leaving police and mobsters alike wondering who would become the new mob patriarch. As with any death, people felt it was the end of an era. Some 400 visitors came to the

the Rhode Island underworld. (Curiously, one of them was the nephew of the two slain Marfeo brothers—possibly he came to gloat.)

There was a Mass—like all mobsters, Patriarca had been a devout Catholic and contributed to the church, buying good publicity and possibly reduced time in the Underworld (the spiritual, one, that is). At the funeral, the FBI, with characteristic doggedness, did a stakeout, taking down the license plate numbers of those in attendance and photographed the "mourners," some of whom had even known the deceased. Among the 300 in attendance, there were mob lawyers, some associates, close relatives, the curious, a crackpot candidate for mayor who said the dead Don had been a "beautiful man" and of course—a group of merciless reporters. Junior gave the reporters a rose on behalf of his dead father.

Breaking with an old tradition, the other big American mobsters stayed away to avoid exposure. The Padrone was buried at the Gate of Heaven cemetery in a dark business suit with rosary beads in one hand. His marble tomb had the name "PATRIARCA" carved on it; below that was a scripture about " life everlasting."

One observer said the corpse looked ten years younger than it was.

POSTSCRIPT

After Patriarca's death, the family ran around, quite literally, like a mad dog with its head lopped off. Unfortunately for the Mafia, Junior, a builder of expensive homes and a clever politician, assumed control, demoting the haughty Angiulo to the status of soldier, and making Zannino head of the Boston franchise; he also raised the brutal William Grasso of New Haven to be his own underboss.

This arrangement didn't last long. Grasso was assassinated (to no one's regret except Junior's), and so the young don, feeling he was losing his grip, decided to appease as many people as possible by "opening the books" and making some new members.

Little did he know the initiation was being recorded by the FBI; like father, like son, at least in one thing—they both got bugged.

Junior, as he spoke to the inductees, must have been a bit sentimental about the good old days of the Patriarca family, when he said the initiates would leave "with what we've had in years past." The FBI matched Junior's voice patterns to a radio show he once foolishly had commented on via phone. Arrested, Junior was tried and sentenced along with the other top bosses of family, leaving no one capable to run the show and setting the stage for opportunists like Stevie Flemmi and Whitey Bulger to move in.

Indeed, there is not much left to show of what was once one of the largest businesses in the northeast, or of Raimondo Patriarca, the treacherous little bootlegger who had become the Don of New England.

chapter four

Jim Fisk, Vermont's greatest clown

Even as Jim Fisk waddled down the stairs of a New York opera house with mortal bullet wounds riddling his fat carcass, he had already proven that his home state of Vermont could create a man whose talents and inclination for stealing and buffoonery were of the first rank in Christendom.

The over-educated and effete Wall Street professionals—such as Michael Milken and Ivan Boesky—who ravaged America's financial infrastructure in the 1980s lacked the color of the Robber Baron scalawags of the post Civil War era. Even by the lax standards of the gilded era, Fisk stood out as an outrageous individual, a radical, nearly anarchic figure who tested the limits of all law and even the fabric of his society. Not for nothing was the Vermont bumpkin known as the "Barnum of Wall Street." Fisk proved that a nobody, if he is clever, greedy and determined enough, can steal as much as one born with all the advantages of high society.

Poetically, Fisk was born on All Fool's Day, 1834 in Bennington, Vermont. His family soon moved to Brattleboro, a small village nestled cozily in Vermont's green landscape, cut in two by a river and surrounded by purplish mountains. Fisk was all-American in many ways: while his formal education was poor, he later apprenticed with some of the greatest con men of all time—an inimitable learning experience.

He had a variety of jobs before he achieved greatness as a thief. He worked as a circus hand, waiter, and flamboyant peddler—ultimately to be his true vocation. His early experiences indeed taught him key things; as circus showman, he learned how to talk to the public at large, draw attention to himself, and seem larger than life—ideal training for a Wall Street huckster, still as true now as it was then.

The Civil War was a great opportunity for Fisk. Like so many other men, he saw the almost unbelievable profits to be made during war, and worked handling Boston-based retailer Jordan Marsh's Civil War wholesale contracts. Using a connection with a congressman, he got a contract to sell blankets and various shoddy goods to the army.

In Washington he lived in an expensive hotel and entertained and bribed government agents sufficiently to make his employer the biggest firm of its kind (nothing ever changes in the nation's capitol). Not one to worry much about causes versus profits, he even purchased smuggled Confederate cotton for a Boston syndicate.

His success soon landed him a partnership with Jordan Marsh; when he got too big, however, they bought him out of the firm, and he tried wholesaling on his own.

ON TO WALL STREET

In 1865, as a dry goods wholesaler, he failed. However, upon hearing of the treaty signed at Appomattox, Fisk became part of a scheme to send an agent to England to sell Confederate bonds short there before the news of the south's surrender arrived. He made money, but soon blew his ill-gotten gains and needed financial rescue.

A man's character is his fate, and thus, eventually, the fledgling con man Fisk became a Wall Street trader. In a short time he was broke. "Wall Street has ruined me," he said, "and Wall Street shall pay for it. □

He met his guru and later partner and nemesis, Daniel Drew, nicknamed colorfully, "The Deacon." Drew was an outrageously shameless rascal and thief, as well as a man of public piety and the founder of the Drew Theological Seminary of New Jersey—hence, his nickname.

Jim Fisk, Vermont's Greatest Clown

Drew, who owned a controlling interest in the Erie Railroad, set up his young protege in a brokerage firm —Fisk and Belden—in 1866. He also made him a director on the Erie Railroad. This was the beginning of an amazing career for a man who could himself make nothing, but was able to manufacture trust in the hearts and minds of his investors. Fisk's firm prospered.

THE WAR FOR THE ERIE

Railroads were the driving economic force of Fisk's day—a source of great wealth to the few speculators who owned and built them, even if they improved the country's transportation only a little. Some men saw railroads as the technology of the future— for Fisk and his colleagues, they were just a way to get rich at the expense of fools.

Fisk joined the Deacon's side in a titanic fight to control the Erie Railroad, "two thin streaks of rust" plagued with accidents, running between the Hudson and Buffalo. With Fisk and Drew was Jay Gould, another epic Wall Street thief. The trio, directors of the railroad, were arrayed against a formidable enemy, the powerful and imperious Robber Baron, "Commodore" Cornelius Vanderbilt (whose lavish "Breakers" mansion can still be seen today in Newport, R.I.).

Vanderbilt was trying to take over the Erie and consolidate it with his other New York lines by cornering its stock in the market. He launched his first assault on February 17, 1868. Faced with opposition from Drew and Gould, the ill-tempered Vanderbilt decided to ruin them all. Learning Fisk was one of Drew's henchmen, Vanderbilt said: "Then we must kill him off. He's too sharp for a greenhorn and too bold for an old hand. I don't know what to make of him." (Nevertheless, Vanderbilt did have a grudging admiration for Fisk—after the Vermonter's murder, the Commodore consulted mediums to get Fisk's ghost to give him stock market tips.)

To stop Vanderbilt from buying up the controlling shares of Erie, Drew and Fisk came up with a novel idea: just keep printing out stock shares so that Vanderbilt would have to keep acquiring them in perpetuity. Fisk was to dub this illegal tactic "the freedom of the press." The worthless stock kept rolling out, and Vanderbilt kept buying it—costing him millions. Fisk, Drew, and Gould made a fortune off the Commodore, who got a court order from their own private judge, George Barnard, to make them stop.

There now started a bizarre battle between various judges in different courts. Fisk asked judge Ransom Balcolm, from a different jurisdiction than Barnard's, to intervene to keep the tyrannical Vanderbilt from taking over the Erie. Balcolm demanded the litigation before Judge Barnard to end. Both courts ruled each other invalid. Meanwhile, Fisk and his cohorts kept issuing watered down stock—which Vanderbilt had to keep buying if he wanted to take over the railroad.

"If this damn printing press don't break down," said Fisk, seeing the humor, "I'll be damned if I don't give the old hog all he wants of Erie."

The trio held a secret meeting and voted to issue $10 million of convertible bonds to be printed on stolen certificates and sell them. "Give us enough rag paper," said Fisk, "and we'll hammer the everlasting tar out of that mariner from Staten Island."

Vanderbilt was puzzled about where these new securities came from; when he learned he had just spent $7 million for illegal stocks, there was nearly a financial panic. Incensed, Barnard issued an arrest warrant for Fisk, Gould, and Drew. To get out of Barnard's jurisdiction, the quick thinking Fisk rowed over the mist-covered waters dividing New York from New Jersey, arriving at the Ladies' Parlor of Taylor's Hotel in Jersey City. Fisk offered a homespun explanation of his thinking:

"Up in Brattleboro in my kid days, I used to see people avoid interviews with the sheriff by crossing the bridge over to Connecticut, and once there they would let the Vermont sheriff whistle for them." An eternal optimist, he noted: "I always did like the air of Jersey."

Fearing kidnap, they fortified the hotel (renamed "Fort Taylor") with guns and ammunition, mounted a cannon on the dock, and summoned militia men, police, thugs, and detectives to protect them. Fisk even took command of a flotilla of four boats loaded with men armed with Springfield rifles.

Like Joseph Kennedy, Fisk knew the value of good public relations and could tell the most outrageous lies without flinching. He also ensured favorable press coverage by treating the reporters covering the struggle to free liquor and cigars, telling them Erie was in the middle of a combat "in the interest of the poorer classes especially."

Fisk said he and his confederates had not fled justice—oh, no rather, they had been forced to leave New York because of the Commodore's spider web of treachery and influence; judge Barnard was merely Vanderbilt's tool. And remember, said Fisk, Vanderbilt made Erie's transportation rates so high that the poor masses of New York were starving for lack of trains to haul grain. Fisk's lies, as well as his greed and cleverness, were always of the first rank.

Both sides were using judges against one another the way average litigants usually employed lawyers. To take it one step higher, Fisk and Gould decided to actually change the laws that prevented them from printing up fraudulent stock. However, as Fisk and Co. offered only a paltry $1,000 in bribe money per legislator, the bill failed. The price was later renegotiated and the bill passed the assembly—despite liberal applications of graft and liquor from Vanderbilt. The full cost of the legislation ran about $500,000 in Erie stockholders' money.

Yet, the stalemate between the two parties continued. Of course, with all the company money being spent on litigation and on Wall Street, there was nothing left over for the dilapidated railroad itself. On April 15, rusty rails on the Erie caused a crash that claimed 40 lives. Neither Fisk's nor Vanderbilt's camp paid any heed to it.

The war between the Drew faction and Vanderbilt couldn't go on forever, and eventually a weak link in the chain emerged. Drew, a pillar of the church who hated scandal and missed his home, began to soften. The Commodore secreted a spy pretending to be a waiter into Fort Taylor who slipped Uncle Drew a note saying: "Come and see me. Van Derbilt." (Yes, he spelled his own name incorrectly.)

Every Sunday the fugitives went back to New York—on Sundays civil criminals were free from arrest. Drew took the opportunity to go Vanderbilt's mansion to hurl himself at his enemy, tears flowing, and cut a deal. However, Drew hadn't reckoned on his pupil Fisk's cunning. Never having trusted his mentor fully, Fisk had sent a detective to shadow Drew, and so got wind of the Deacon's treachery.

Outraged, Fisk discovered that Drew had taken Erie funds with him over the river to New York, and got a judge to seize whatever money the Deacon had left in Jersey City. When the two met, Drew said he felt Erie money was unsafe in the hotel; Fisk said he felt Drew's money had been unsafe, too, and so had that attached. The pupil had one-upped his guru, whose jaw now hung open with discovery.

Despite the Deacon's defection, Fisk wanted to fight on. He told his mistress, Josie Mansfield, that: "It was either a Fisk palace in New York or a stone palace at Sing Sing." ("Sing Sing" was the New York state prison at Ossining.) He also told Josie that if he was imprisoned, she should live near him and make him "rusty iron garlands of roses."

Fisk and some of the other directors, each suspecting the others of treachery, finally decided to pay a visit to the Commodore. While dressing, Vanderbilt told Fisk that unless Fisk bought back 100,000 shares of diluted stock from him, he would ensure that the directors of Erie remained criminals in New York.

Fisk later claimed Vanderbilt threatened he would "keep his bloodhounds on us, and pursue us until we took his stock off his hands; he would be damned if he would keep it." However, Fisk replied to Vanderbilt he would be damned if he bought the worthless paper back. Striking a moral note, the Vermont bumpkin said he would not allow Vanderbilt to rob the railroad, and said he was "thunderstruck and dumbfounded that our directors, whom I had supposed respectable men, would have had anything to do with such proceedings."

In the end, though, they all cut a deal. The contempt charges evaporated; the trio kept their gains from selling the Erie stock; and Fisk and Gould took control of the railroad from Drew—whom they later destroyed. Although he no right to do so, Vanderbilt took $9 million out of the Erie treasury to cover his losses.

Fisk later said "I told Gould we had sold ourselves to the Devil...after once the Devil had hold of me I kept on signing....I went with the robbers then and I have been with them ever since."

THE GAME GOES ON

Suddenly, Fisk said he was concerned about the maintenance of the railroad. Accidents had happened because of the poor state of the lines. Fisk said "our need for money became more pressing. I did not stop to run and ask my mother how I should get it—the first thing was to get it—get it...."

To punish the Fisk and Gould duo, Vanderbilt lowered the shipping costs on his other railroad, the New York Central, to under one dollar a head for cattle. Gould and the Vermont trickster simply bought up cattle and started shipping them on Vanderbilt's line and made more profits for themselves. Vanderbilt nearly lost his mind with rage and then decided he had better let the two upstarts alone.

In need of a war chest, Gould & Fisk came up with yet another swindle. Erie happened to have a contract with the United States Express Company for carrying goods. Fisk now told United States Express the cost of shipping was going up by half a million dollars annually; the express company said they couldn't pay the difference.

Fisk and Gould now publicly announced they were creating their own express company. Not surprisingly, the stock of the United States Express plummeted from $60 a share to $16. Fisk and Gould then started buying this devalued stock up at a bargain price before signing a new contract with the company. After the new deal, United States Express' stock began to rise, and at this point, they sold their stock and made a $3 million profit. Hungry for even greater loot, Gould and Fisk now dumped the once worthless stock from Vanderbilt at $70 a share, making another $3.5 million profit.

Now it came time to elect the officers of the railroad. On August 10, 1868, the company declared the stock transfer books closed for the election, and only those who owned shares as of August 19 would be allowed to vote. That date was no accident—Gould and Fisk knew they and their colleagues would have a majority of shares through that day. They took these shares and went back to Wall Street to gamble with them, at the same time voting themselves back into office.

Their triumph was complete. On October 13, 1868, the board elected Gould president and director and Fisk director and comptroller. William Tweed, the infamously corrupt Tammany Hall politician, also became a director—after all, Fisk and Gould knew they might need some political assistance. The corrupt state senator Tweed said Fisk and Gould's election hijinks would ensure that "experienced and intelligent management" would stay in charge and prevent Erie from being "a mere creature of Wall Street speculation."

The stage was now set for truly epic skullduggery. The Erie Railroad was cradling life-sucking parasites inside it—men who would virtually drive the business to extinction.

Drew, Gould and Fisk put some $14 million of their ill gotten gains from the sale of the dubious Erie stock into a number of banks; they then demanded to withdraw the money, triggering a money shortage. The banks had to call in outstanding loans; the national economy suddenly froze; Wall Street went into upheaval and stocks crashed. The trio now took the chance to buy up batches of Erie stock very cheaply. They made a killing—and killed the financial health of hundreds of others in the process.

Speculation with the stock continued. At one point, Drew was facing ruination because Fisk was manipulating the stock higher and higher. A noted actor without shame when it came to trying to steal money, he went to Fisk, weeping, and begged him to stop. That did no good. Next he then threatened to swear out an affidavit to have Fisk and Gould expelled from Erie. Nothing helped; Fisk and Gould ruined Drew, who was never again a Wall Street baron.

THE PRINCE OF THE ERIE

Fisk, as an important officer at Erie, knew how to live the high life. He began to use company money to not only take care of basic business functions like bribing public officials, but also to fund lavish Broadway shows and, of course, live the elevated life of a playboy. His mistress, the famed and notorious "actress," Helen Josie Mansfield, was, according to the corpulent standards of the time, a voluptuous looking beauty.

After meeting her and paying her overdue rent, he eventually moved her into lodgings in fashionable Broadway. He also showed some vanity and began to wax his mustache. He later put her on Erie's payroll for $1,000—for services clearly rendered only to him. She was also marvelously treacherous and greedy, loved to spend Fisk's money, and although she claimed to be 24, she was about 30. Little did Fisk know it, but was in effect, courting his own death.

Despite his affair with Josie, whom he called "Dumpling" and "Lumpsum"—she always wanted her cash up front and in one lump—he remained publicly fond of his wife, Lucy. Fisk said "she always telegraphs me when she's coming, and I clean up and have a warm welcome for her."

His behavior didn't escape public notice—nor did he want it to—and he was dubbed "Prince of the Erie." While the older Wall Street money culture despised him as a bumpkin, Fisk could have cared less how people viewed him—he was, after all, laughing his way to the bank.

Whiskey and women appeared to be so prominent a part of his life that master criminal Deacon Drew—who saw nothing wrong with stealing and lying but everything wrong with extramarital sex— told Fisk to repent.

"No, Uncle," replied Fisk, "there isn't any hope for Jim Fisk. I'm a gone goose....I was born to be bad....I'm having a good time now and I've got to pay for it hereafter, why, I suppose it's no more than fair shakes: and I'll take what's coming to me."

He added that "I don't make any bones of saying that I like these scarlet women—they're approachable...."

The Deacon wasn't alone in casting a grim look at "Jubilee Jim"; the Vermonter was universally denounced as a sensual rogue. One stockholder even threatened to sue because, as Erie's Prince, Fisk was harming the railroad's reputation by appearing with females of "bad repute." Fisk was no drunk, however; like Joseph Kennedy, despite how much liquor Fisk dispensed, he was a teetotaler.

He was quick with down-home, folksy sayings. When asked where some of the huge stock market sums he played with vanished to he would reply: "It went where the woodbine twineth."

Interestingly, while he could steal without a flinch, poverty moved him. Fisk distributed coal and flour to needy families at his own expense, and made sure his charity never made the papers. When a friend from Boston broke his neck swimming, Fisk took care of his widow and provided for his daughters' educations. Fisk even became the sponsor of a black church on Eighth Avenue, claiming it was "damned hard" to have too much piety.

His humor, even when distributing charity, was unflagging. When members of the Brattleboro Baptist Church asked him for money for a new fence around the church cemetery, Fisk asked them why the project was necessary. He reasoned: "Those that are in can't get out; and those that are out don't want to get in...." He still gave $500—a sum that turned out to be an investment in his future resting place.

One writer, Samuel Bowles, editor of the Massachusetts *Springfield Republican* (considered the premier newspaper in the state), described Fisk thus: "He is almost as broad as he is high, and so round that he rolls rather than walks. But his nervous energy is stimulated rather than deadened by his fat...." He also said: "Many of his friends predict him for the state prison or the lunatic asylum; his father is already in the latter."

The good-natured Falstaffian Fisk was usually more amused than outraged by the verbal jabs that came at him from the press. But Bowles' outburst about his father broke through Fisk's jolly tolerance and he sued the editor for criminal libel. The New York police arrested Bowles.

Amazingly, Fisk the crook used the courts to his best advantage. At Erie, litigation was a way of life, a virtual full time job for both Gould and the Prince of Erie. Fisk retained one lawyer whose job it was to monitor the actions of all of his other lawyers and report on their status. "The lawyers lap up Erie money like kittens lap up milk," he said.

The Vermont speculator mastered the art of the lawsuit, realizing how he could buy precious time to find legal loopholes and continue with his shenanigans unmolested. Fisk was so plagued by process servers he built a special passageway from the Grand Opera House to his own home to keep them from bothering him.

It was through legal mumbo-jumbo that Fisk and Gould kept a group of English investors who owned half of Erie's stock from voting it. To further their stranglehold on the company even more, the duo even introduced the Erie Classification Bill—which allowed top tier officers like Fisk and Gould to hold their positions for five years at time! So much the worse for the railroad.

They distributed graft liberally in the form of loans, gifts, stock, furniture, etc. Although Tweed was a director of the railroad, he was hired for his assistance; on the books, bribes were listed as "legal expenses." Fisk's friend in the courts, Judge Barnard, owned Erie stock; Fisk even sent him two stuffed owls to acknowledge the man's legal wisdom.

Yet, no dividend was issued and the company's debts mounted. So mismanaged was the company, one Wall Street maven said, "On the day Erie declares a dividend, icicles will freeze in hell." When a fire broke out in the Erie headquarters,

Wall Streeters said it was from the overworked presses getting too hot printing bad stock. And although Gould and Fisk churned out $53,425,700 of stock, they refused to sink a paltry $6 million into the railroad to make it safe for travel.

No doubt wanting to have some fun, be in the limelight, and have unlimited access to beautiful starlets, in December, 1868 Fisk, using Erie money, bought Pike's Opera House. It was an act of singular financial idiocy—he was only a stock market swindler, not an artist. Then, seeking a headquarters for the Erie commensurate with his sense of greatness, he acquired the Grand Opera House for $820,000. He now demonstrated some real talent for shoddy grandeur, setting hundreds of workmen loose to renovate it. When complete, the Grand Opera was an epic monstrosity, full of carved woodwork, stained glass, and paintings—and, of course, the basement held a printing press from whence he could issue his shoddy financial instruments, as the need arose.

For security, the management hired a local street thug, Tommy Lynch, and his gang to protect "Castle Erie." The gangsters kept at bay process servers, stockholders, or any victims of the railroad's all too frequent and avoidable accidents. Anyone who went to the courts had to deal with the corrupt Tammany Hall judges on Fisk's payroll; when one disgruntled Erie investor kept pressing a suit against the company, an annoyed judge Barnard fined him $5000 for contempt.

THE ARTIST

Although he had little talent as impresario, Fisk insisted on directing the shows he put on. Ever the clown, he wanted to stage opera buffa. He fired one manager who, while dressed as an Indian, wanted to take his tomahawk and brain him with it. Although he tried to bribe reviewers to give him good press, he failed, and had to cut his ticket prices in half to gain viewers.

"A more obnoxious individual never imposed himself upon the stage," said one critic.

Because he was well known for defrauding European investors, he had problems getting continental artists to help him. Confusing extravagance and exaggeration with beauty, Fisk made all sorts of outrageous things happen on stage—sometimes a Fisk show would have a different cast each act!

He could be an obstreperous director. At one point, a conductor left his stand during rehearsal and struck Fisk on the nose, starting a brawl—Fisk gave the conductor a black eye.

It is worth noting he did launch one success, "The Twelve Temptations," replete with long legged dancers; each succeeding night he alternated between blondes and brunettes. The bottom of the playbill said that although it had 100 beautiful ladies, a grand transformation scene, and terpsichorean aerostatics, it "contains nothing objectionable."

NOTHING LOST SAVE HONOR

Instead of repairing the dilapidated and now dangerous Erie Railroad line, Fisk and company set about to rob another one—the Albany & Susquehanna Line. This battle got bitter—eventually one end of the railroad was in Fisk's hands, the other in his enemy's. Two judges, both bought and paid for by the warring factions, declared each other's rulings illegal. A seesaw conflict erupted with injunctions flying over telegraph wires and sheriffs running to and from to execute the courts' commands. During a dispute over some of the contested rail line, two trains collided head on and soldiers from either side started fighting among the wreck.

At one point, when combat broke out between the two camps, the sheriff trying to intervene was unsure which judge's orders to obey. The unflappable Fisk, cracking jokes and dispensing champagne, assured the sheriff he should follow Judge Barnard's dictates. Eventually, Fisk strayed into contempt of court; in Albany he was even bodily thrown down a flight of stairs onto the sidewalk.

Defeated, he got ready for another raid and said, amused: "Nothing is lost save honor. "

Regrettably for Fisk, he chanced to make the acquaintance of his future murderer, the handsome young Ned Stokes, and took such a liking to him he introduced him to Josie and even named a canary after him. Fisk set Stokes up as a treasurer of the Brooklyn Oil Refinery—Brooklyn Oil got discounts on the Erie rail line, and in turn, the railroad bought a lot of its oil.

ADMIRAL AND COLONEL

Fisk's career took an even odder turn when he bought the controlling interest in the Narragansett Steamship Company. This concern had two ferries, the Providence and the Bristol, which traveled the waters between Fall River and New York City.

He decided to become not only shipbuilder, but a commander of a fleet. He commissioned two new huge boats for traveling the Hudson River: one ferry was called the *Jay Gould*—the second, and, naturally, the larger of the two—steamboats he called the *James Fisk, Jr.* Each ship had a portrait of its namesake hung inside. Fisk, with an eye for catching public attention, installed bands on the boats, and even bought 250 canaries and put one in every stateroom. The birds all had names such as "General Grant" and "Jeff Davis."

Going a step further, Fisk decked himself out in a blue uniform patterned after that of a U.S. Navy admiral. He even added some new phrases to his repertoire of homey sayings: "Well shiver my mizzen-mast and rip my royal halyards."

One of his never-ending indulgences was the building of a new locomotive—one of the few capital investments made in a railroad by Fisk—hung it with oil paintings, and named it the *George C. Barnard* after the corrupt judge .

Traveling further down the military vein, Fisk , who stayed comfortably out of the Civil War to make money, in 1870 secured the commission of colonel for himself in the 9th Regiment of the

New York militia by paying off the unit's rather large debts. Training in the heat at "Camp Gould" often stopped so the men could have beer. Fisk's excursions with the troops were lavish affairs filled with free champagne for his troops, during these grave military operations, he was fond of taking his meals at expensive restaurants.

During one maneuver, a constable presented Fisk with a court summons for an unpaid $41.25 grocer bill for butter. Fisk stomped on the summons. "It is a trick to insult me in front of my men," he said, and his men surrounded the unlucky constable, forcing him to flee.

While watching a chorus show with ladies kicking their feet over the heads, he said: "That is one movement the Ninth cannot perform, I'll bet." Fisk met opposition when he tried to march in a Bunker Hill Day celebration in Boston. When the mayor and city council tried to stop Fisk from holding a prayer on Boston Common, he said, "When the Ninth Regiment wants to pray, I'm damned if it won't do it." Nevertheless, his lavish band drew a crowd of 50,000 onlookers.

BLACK FRIDAY

In 1869, Jim Fisk, Jr. changed the course of the world economy almost single-handedly through a foolhardy scheme to corner the world's gold supply—then a crucial financial resource for businessmen. "There is a certain amount of fictitiousness about the prosperity of the country," Fisk rationalized, "and the bubble might as well be tapped in one way as another."

Fisk and, as always, his partner Gould needed to buy more gold—through contracts —than the $100 million there was in the national treasury—all the buying would drive the price of gold up. When they had enough contracts, they would call for delivery of the gold; the sellers would be unable to comply, and then Gould and Fisk would sell of their contracts and flee. They needed to know how the government would react—if the government sold off too much gold to stabilize the market, it would depress the price and the plan would go bust.

He and Gould set the stage in June. Then, dressed in his smart uniform, complete with kid gloves and a diamond to hold his tie in place, Fisk welcomed president Ulysses Grant aboard the well scrubbed and gleaming *Providence*. A band played, the crowd cheered and cannons boomed as the astonishingly corrupt Grant, along with Secretary of the Treasury George Boutwell, became Fisk's guests.

Fisk, who radiated his characteristic ease, tried to probe Grant's position on gold; Grant was vague. But after the meeting, Gould and Fisk, influenced by Grant's scheming, dishonest brother in law, Abel R. Corbin, decided the president would not sell off the U.S. gold deposits and thus crash gold's price. They continued scheming....Fisk bribed some newspapermen to write stories claiming the government wouldn't sell off its gold.

Meanwhile, on July 14, yet another disaster befell Erie when an engineer fell asleep at a crossroads while a train was passing him by. The engineer awoke, and thinking the other locomotive train had gone on, steered into it and crashed. Nine people burned to death, including a minister who died while rescuers were trying to free him from the wreckage. With his usual callousness, Fisk blamed the accident on the "villainy" of a halfwit named Bowen and the incompetent engineer.

They had more important things to attend to, like the ruination of the world's economy. Gould and Fisk proceeded with the attempt to secure a monopoly on gold. Fisk started buying, propping up the price of gold artificially. He had a big line of credit, using the Tenth National Bank as his creditor—after all, he and Gould owned a controlling interest in the institution.

Stocks began to drop in value and money became scarce as people bought up gold. The public began to plead for Washington to sell off its gold and forestall financial disaster. When Fisk learned that gold had closed at 144, he celebrated with a cigar. It looked as if his scheme was coming to fruition.

On the other hand, Gould, quietly realizing the foolhardiness of their position, began to secretly sell off his contracts.

September 24, 1869 became known as Black Friday, when half of Wall Street crashed. Things were overheated—Fisk claimed he would make the price go up to 200. That's when Washington started selling its gold. The price dropped to 135, and a horde of speculators were ruined. Even Fisk was bankrupt —at least on paper. A lynch mob roamed Wall Street looking for the two scoundrels, Fisk and Gould; a gang of speculators even broke into Gould's brokerage house, but the wily trickster had already fled through a side door.

Fisk became the "goat" of Black Friday, and hid in his opera house, claiming he feared hanging. Of course, Fisk blamed "that damned old scoundrel," Corbin. "I suspect that the whole thing was a damned trick from beginning to end...." The conspirators, he noted, were "forty miles down the Delaware" with each man dragging out his own corpse. Later, he said: "A fellow can't have a little innocent fun without everybody raising a halloo and going wild."

The effects of Black Friday were felt in businesses throughout the country—and even in Europe. At the rumor someone had shot Fisk down, there was public cheering—at the trendy New York restaurant, Delmonico's, people drank toasts.

THE ROAD DOWN

Hereafter, things went badly for Fisk. As the rich often do, he tried rehabilitating his image with public acts of charity, even driving a wagon loaded with supplies to Chicago after the city's disastrous fire in 1871.

That summer, the city's Catholic Irish started rioting against the marching Protestant Orangemen. The governor called the Ninth out; facing down the rioting Irish, they militia opened fire and killed and wounded many in the crowd. Someone hit Fisk with a chunk of iron and his own men trampled on their colonel, leaving him with a dislocated ankle.

When the angry crowd spotted him hiding indoors, someone said: "That damned Fisk is in there. Kill the villain! Hang him!" Fisk fled through back alleys, leaving his men behind, two of whom were mortally wounded. He only got away by disguising himself in a moldy coat and hat. While fleeing, he saw Gould, with whom he was still good friends—the Erie was more valuable than pride and Fisk liked a clever swindler—driving by and demanded a ride.

Gould took him to the Continental restaurant, where Fisk was fanned by an attractive lady. Although Fisk claimed he had fled to spare his men the dreaded sight of their commander wounded, the *Times* said that Fisk "has shown that he can fight and pray, and when needful, run away in a manner surpassed by few soldiers of any age."

Things were going bad at the Erie, as well. A locomotive exploded, and in New Jersey, rotten rails gave way while a freight train was riding on them and the train was wrecked. Another engine jumped track at Hackensack and crushed a fireman's foot. On December 31, 1871 Fisk resigned as vice-president of Erie, but retained his position as comptroller and director.

Unfortunately for Fisk, his mistress Josie now fell in love with the handsome Stokes, and began to find Fisk contemptible. She wouldn't even let him leave his rubber galoshes at her house, he complained. Fisk wrote a goodbye letter to her.

"Like the Arabs, we will fold our tents and quietly steal away, and when we spread them next we hope it will be where the 'woodbine twineth,' over the river Jordan on the beautiful banks of Heaven." She gave Stokes the letters; together they threatened to publish them and make Fisk a greater laughingstock than he already was. Eventually, the two rivals, Fisk and Stokes, appeared before Josie. She tried to patch things up.

"It won't do, Josie," said Fisk. "You can't run two engines on one track in contrary directions at the same time."

Now Fisk tried to ruin Stokes: he took away an Erie contract for Stokes' oil refinery and ordered his arrest for embezzlement. He talked about having a street thug "put him out of the way" for $500. Stokes sued Fisk for conspiracy to ruin his business; Fisk then accused Stokes and Josie of blackmail; they sued him for libel and perjury.

Stokes began to feel desperate, and hearing of a coming indictment for blackmail, for both business and personal reasons, decided to put an end to Fisk's life. On January 6, 1872, Stokes, armed with a pistol, cornered Fisk on a staircase in the Opera House.

"I've got you now," said Stokes. He fired twice.

Shot at point blank range, Fisk said: "For God's sake will anybody save me?" He staggered and clutched the railing, but didn't fall; Stokes fled through an upstairs corridor and was arrested in a barber shop. Shot above his navel and with blood pouring from his arm, Fisk walked down the staircase.

"I am not afraid to die, but then if I am going to die I would like to know beforehand," he said. "I feel just as I used to feel when I filled myself with green apples. I've got a belly-ache."

His loyal wife came to him, and approached his bed as he died, kissing him at 10:45 p.m. "My dear boy!" she said. "He was such a good boy." That summed the man up perfectly—even the normally cold Gould wept uncontrollably—he had lost his better, jollier half.

AFTERMATH

Responses to his murder varied. The furor surrounding Jubilee Jim's death reminded people of Lincoln's assassination. Many were grief stricken—after all, they had just lost the best show in town. By coincidence, a respected member of the stock exchange, Henry Heise, died at the same time as Fisk; there was hesitation about lowering the flag to half-mast, lest the show of grief by attributed to the deceased bumpkin.

With Fisk gone, speculators assumed the management of Erie had to improve, and so its stock went up by four and a half percent. Although Gould later maintained that his partner's demise ended the era of bad management at Erie, there were no longer any fools credulous enough to believe him.

Fisk, in great pomp and circumstance was taken to the grave under the Ninth's colors and buried in his colonel's uniform. The minister presiding over the funeral in Brattleboro prayed no less then a half hour for Fisk...his family...the regiment... Brattleboro ... the United States... The service ended in hysterics.

Yet there was still humor in the wake of the rascal's death. The *Vermont Free Press* declared with Yankee stoicism: "He made a nice, quiet corpse."

Horace Greeley summed Fisk up best: "When he devoured the widow's substance he differed from so many of his associates in refraining from the pretense of long prayers."

The Rev. Henry Ward Beecher (himself a hypocrite guilty of adultery) said that "God's providence struck him to the ground!" He added: "Mark the end of this wicked man, and turn back again to the ways of integrity."(He should have lived to see Kennedy's rise.)

Hate turned to remorse: A ballad was composed to celebrate the colorful scoundrel whose antics New York now sorely missed. A month after the slaying, Fisk's 250 canaries were sold off—the one named Colonel James Fisk, Jr., brought a whopping $16.25, the one named Edward Stokes going for a mere $7.50.

Stokes himself did jail time, then lived on modestly until his death at 61; Josie, the cause of Fisk's death, herself died impoverished and forgotten.

True to their own, Brattleboro collected $425,000 and built their favorite son a monument, complete with four scantily clad women to adorn it. Fisk himself would have had to laugh.

Epilogue: In 1942, after a huge battle and major reorganization, the Erie Railroad declared its first dividend in 69 years.

chapter five

the pious samuel adams

Samuel Adams would use anything to achieve his goals — terrorism, libel, extortion, ridicule—even prayer.

It was in September, 1768, at the height of the agitation between Colonial Massachusetts and King George III of England. The political climate had heated up between the mother country and her colony and things had started getting bloody. Royal governor Thomas Hutchinson had forbade the general court from meeting; the king's warships sailed in the harbor and the dreaded English army was about disembark at Boston's wharves. While at a hastily called Boston town meeting, Adams came up with a master stroke of rebellion.

The authorities stood ready to arrest Adams and his cohorts and hang them for treason. Now Adams and his friend, the brilliant, lunatic lawyer James Otis, urged everyone to arm themselves for "great danger."

"Have you not heard," said Adams with mock gravity, lying without shame, "we arm against a French fleet, coming down from Halifax." Everyone laughed. Adams held up his hand. The great propagandist and Puritan had yet to unsheathe his weapon: desperately, he urged his fellow citizens to fight back at the crown with a weapon that was virtually unstoppable: a day of prayer. The mood of the town meeting was comical—but they voted yes, anyway. Adams indeed had come up with a stroke of near genius. The day of prayer would keep going the momentum of the slowly growing rebellion—in much the same way Mahatma Gandhi would do with his fast days and nonviolent resistance in India.

The English saw Adams' day of prayer for what it was—as nothing less than a sham, an act of criminal rebellion. But it succeeded.

Yes, Adams was a great rabble rouser. It was his single talent in the world. "Put your enemy in the wrong and keep him there," he once said. Adams, one of America's earliest and greatest "spin doctors" and rogues, was a failure at everything in life except making trouble. His ceaseless ranting and raving against the English government ultimately resulted in the American Revolution—and certainly his actions came from all the wrong reasons. Remarkably, for a man renowned for piety, he had not one morsel of integrity or honesty in his fanatical pursuit of rebellion.

A TALENT FOR FAILURE

The future "Dictator" of Boston was a scion of a prominent family, whose history in Massachusetts began in 1630 on the same plot of land in Quincy as Morton's Merry Mount. He was born in 1722 in Boston, a small village of some 8,000. His father, also named Samuel, was a church deacon and successful businessman. However, the deacon's financial acuteness and thrift didn't rub off on the son, unfortunately for Adams—and later the English authorities, who bore the brunt of his resentment at his failure.

As was customary for a young man of property, he attended Harvard. Caught drinking rum, he paid a five pound fine. Eventually, family funds became scarce, and he had to become a waiter in the college dining hall. To please his father, he studied law; to please his mother, he dropped the law, graduating in 1740, and taking his master's in 1743. His dissertation at school advocated fighting "the Supreme Magistrate" if it was necessary. He also got just enough of a taste of philosophy to be dangerous—his later political experience never dislodged his bookish notions about statecraft.

His early, ill-fated business ventures showed promise of the brilliant failure he was to become later. First, Adams borrowed 1,000 pounds from his father, loaning half to a friend, who never paid him back. He managed to lose the rest on his own. He then joined the family brewery, where his incompetence did only modest damage.

After his parents died, Adams took possession of the family house on Purchase Street, along with the brewery. It took ten years for Adams' knack for failure to ruin the brewery and the family fortune; three times sheriffs had tried to auction the house, but each time the city had refused to buy it. Indeed, Adams once launched a propaganda campaign so fierce against the commissioners chasing him for money he got them fired.

A TRUE CALLING

Useless as a merchant, he turned to politics. Adams, the son of a politician, had a gift for scheming and organizing people to his side and forming coalitions. He had a pleasant speaking voice, and even organized a singing society—which of course became another forum for his revolutionary agitation.

He was of average height, with a pleasant face—a key to a political career. He had a fair complexion, with dark blue eyes set under heavy brows. John Singleton Copley's portrait of Adams—commissioned by Adams' off and on again friend, John Hancock—shows a man with thoughtful, defiant brown eyes, thin resolute lips, and narrow but straight shoulders, about to expound on his hatred of the longsuffering English government in the jittery voice he worked so hard to control.

In some ways, with his hostility to the English government and its worldly ways, Adams was a true heir of zealot Puritans Cotton Mather and John Winthrop. Endowed with a generous sense of the righteousness of his own cause and the evil of any enemy's, he treated all adversaries as nothing less than colleagues of Satan. He forbade his dishonest attacks on them from troubling his conscience. Although he was a genuine Puritan fanatic in many ways, the commandment "Thou shalt not lie" never took hold in him; truth couldn't stand in the way of a good piece of propaganda.

Despite being a born zealot and hot headed in temperament, he learned to always seem calm and never let disagreement or insult rile him—another political necessity. He knew that in politics, it is slow and steady that wins, and he would rather hack down the authorities by a murder of a thousand cuts (or slogans) than risk everything on one killer thrust. Sometimes, however, when excited, his hands and head would tremble—indicating the volcano deep within ready to erupt.

His younger cousin and future president, John Adams of nearby Braintree, said of Samuel that he was "zealous, ardent and keen in the Cause, is always for Softness, and Delicacy, and Prudence where they will do, but is stanch and stiff and strict and rigid and inflexible in the Cause....it should be admitted that he is too attentive to the Public and not enough so, to himself and his family."

Indeed, his devotion to politics insured he was a thorough failure as provider to his two wives—both of whom were named Elizabeth (the first he married in 1749, but she died in 1757, the second marrying him in 1764) and two children.

Despite his Puritanism and observance of Sunday religious meetings, Adams did like to live and entertain well. As his sharp eyed cousin said: "He affects to despize Riches, and not to dread Poverty. But no Man is more ambitious of entertaining his Friends handsomely, or of making a decent, an elegant Appearance than he." Adams even redid his house with new paint and wallpaper to please his guests and make them feel at home.

Back then, without television or radio, politicians had to actually go out and meet the people they wanted to vote for them. So, Adams was often seen scurrying around the streets of Boston in his ragged brown coat and rumpled wig, talking to acquaintances, always with a mind to building coalitions and gathering votes.

He befriended men in the street—carpenters, dock workers, and so on. He spent much time in taverns—a place where his cousin John observed "bastards, and legislatories are frequently begotten"— listening to the aggravations and complaints of those whom he would shape into his own private mob—an indispensable tool for any rabble rousing revolutionary. No one knew the average working people like he.

He enjoyed the slow steady career of a professional politician, rising up the ranks on position and committee at a time. He was member of every political organization in Boston; he took every municipal job: town scavenger (which paid him a wage) chimney warden, fire inspector, school committee member, and more.

In 1756, he became tax collector for the city, demonstrating he could fail in public service as effectively as he could in private enterprise. For starters, as tax collector he was well-liked—proving he was the wrong man for the job. He bungled the collection process completely, accepting any excuse to put off taking any taxpayer's funds—but that may have been his intention all along. After all the people whose taxes he neglected to collect would remember his mercy and support his political moves. This was exactly the mob he wanted to mobilize for his own ends.

His laxness in collecting—and handing over—taxes meant that he personally was responsible for the unpaid debt to the city. After eight years, he was in arrears 8,000 pounds and even facing jail for embezzlement. Despite his incompetence—and possible criminal malfeasance—the clever street politician was re-elected yet again.

THE CALL TO ACTION

Adams was to make his true career enticing the citizens of Massachusetts and the other colonies to overthrow the English government—based on grievances more imagined than real. For 10 years, he almost single-handedly kept the cause of revolution alive.

Adams had the advantage of being a political insider. In 1763 he joined the powerful Caucus Club, a group of small merchants and laborers who met at the Green Dragon Tavern, and while drinking rum and smoking tobacco, decided how the town meeting would vote. Adams thus became Boston's first ward boss—a stringpuller on a par with Kennedy or Curley—and later a virtual dictator in Boston, dispensing jobs and throwing around influence for his pet causes.

Otis and Adams made a powerful pair. The duo boasted they had single handedly kicked three royal governors out of the colony. Both were effective orators and skilled at manipulating the public; an extra advantage, Adams was a skilled newspaper propagandist. Not only did he stage events, he shaped the public's perception of them with his newspaper columns, pamphlets, speeches and so on.

Adams was clever enough to always seem distant to what was going on publicly; the riots, threats, and violence he instigated always occurred near him, but no one could ever prove he had caused them. He covered his tracks, cutting his letters into small pieces in the summer and burning them in the winter—he could have taught modern politicians a thing or two about avoiding capture.

In 1765, the English, reasonably attempting to recover what they had spent defending the American colonies in the French and Indian Wars, passed the Stamp Act. This legislation required every business and legal transaction be validated by a prestamped document. Adams, who had been denouncing England in print since 1748 under a variety of pseudonyms, sensed a chance for fame and redemption from his failure by attacking this new tax.

Adams, whose task it was to instruct Boston's legislators how to vote in the General Court, demanded legislators ignore and oppose the Stamp Act. He even now took the opportunity to take a swipe at the hated lieutenant governor and chief justice, Thomas Hutchinson. Not only did Adams resent the elegant and learned Hutchinson on principle as an abler and more refined man than himself, but worse, he bore the man a personal grudge. Hutchinson had dissolved a shaky institution that Adams' father had invested in, the Land Bank, thus harming the Adams family's finances, earning Samuel's resentment forever. Adams and Otis now claimed Hutchinson was behind the stamp act, and had betrayed them.

The Pious Samuel Adams

Adams, with his zeal for fighting any enemy real or imagined, now instructed Boston's representatives to pass a law to deny a salary to any judge that held two jobs—as well as anyone on the governor's council or in the house of representatives who had been appointed to the job by the king. On both counts, Adams was singling Hutchinson out and settling his old vendetta. Like mayor Michael Curley centuries later, Adams could with pinpoint accuracy, use legislation to attack an enemy.

Adams' activities didn't go unnoticed by the king's officials, but they did nothing for the time being—Adams was a powerful and popular man not to be crossed casually. Nevertheless, they held him in contempt, a man with no respect for money, vulgar and shabby, a malcontent only skilled at failure. Hutchinson, who eventually even tried to bribe Adams to silence him, once noted "I doubt whether there is a greater incendiary in the King's dominion...." Eventually the crown would put a price on Adams's head. By then, it was too late.

The same year as the Stamp Act, Adams became a member of the lower chamber of the Massachusetts legislature (or General Court), and its clerk in 1766. In that position, he could truly annoy the hated Hutchinson, as well as royal governor Francis Bernard, whom he later drove out of the colony.

It was about this time that Adams, ever fighting at the sense of inferiority that ate away at him, made the cause of separation from England his major cause in life. To be fair, as a Puritan, he considered the cosmopolitan England a corrupted, effeminate land, lacking spiritual purity—he probably had a point, too. He also had a secret dream: to create a state like ancient Greece had in Sparta, something he had read about in writer Plutarch's *Lives*. Shrewdly, he limited his public attacks on England's parliament, never denouncing the king, all the while privately building up support to overthrow the crown.

As a good politician, Adams also knew how to recruit and then subjugate talent—men like John Hancock, his cousin John Adams, and Otis, and use them to his best advantage. Naturally, Adams become an outspoken leader of the radical element in the legislature, and in 1766, made sure he and his cronies took control of the house, pushing Hutchinson as well as four other Tories, or men loyal to King George, out.

His plans required street muscle, so with Hancock, the richest, shiftiest and shadiest merchant in the colony, Adams recruited from the streets and from the Caucus Club his own private gang of thugs—the Sons of Liberty—a misnomer if there ever was one. The group had much in common with Hitler's Black Shirts or Raymond Patriarca's Mafia thugs. Picked from the fertile fields of volatile Boston's riff-raff, the Sons of Liberty denied freedom of dissent for their opponents. They bullied, threatened and hurt anyone who didn't obey their secret masters.

The Machiavellian Adams, like Lenin, Ghandi, Mao, and other revolutionaries, knew how to stir the public—or mob—to serve his own ends. As time wore on, the Sons and Hancock became the financial supporters of Adams and his household—Adams, after all had better things to do than take care of his family, like annoy the English.

On August 14, the Sons hung in effigy Andrew Oliver, a Massachusetts supreme court justice and Hutchinson's brother-in-law, and a large boot—standing in for the English Lord Bute. The two objects dangled from an elm in downtown Boston on what would be called the "Liberty Tree." (Another misnomer.) That night, a mob crying "Liberty, Property, and no Stamps!" broke into Oliver's town house and destroyed the place.

The next day, while standing under the ill-named Liberty Tree, Adams pretended to be shocked about the incident. When someone asked who was responsible, he replied, "I wonder indeed. I must inquire." He blamed Hutchinson, asking if the man's infuriating nepotism were "not enough to excite Jealousies among the People?"

Oliver, terrified, resigned. But that wasn't enough for Adams and his private Mafia. While Hutchinson ate supper with his family in their elegant North End mansion, a group of screaming and yelling thugs, armed with axes, appeared at the doorstep. This "hellish crew," as Hutchinson dubbed them, smashed the front door down, then chased the lieutenant governor and his family out of their home, and proceeded to demolish and plunder it until morning with the "rage of devils." Hutchinson barely escaped with his life; the Sons even cut his fruit trees down.

Adams was responsible for this terrorism, although in public he half-heartedly denounced it. After all, he noted, lying more boldly than usual, some of the papers found in the mansion proved Hutchinson had indeed concocted the Stamp Act. In December, the Sons forced the elderly Oliver to stand in the rain at the Liberty Tree and publicly resign his job as stamp distributor.

THE TOWNSEND ACTS

Although the English parliament repealed the Stamp Tax in 1767, they blundered again by passing another annoying set of small and annoying tariffs called the Townsend Acts. This law tacked minor fees on glass, paper, and tea. Had the Parliament been more astute and not passed so many taxes guaranteed to outrage their colonies, Adams would have passed his life away as just another big-city political hack.

Tax collectors (except Adams himself) have never been popular, but the Sons of Liberty took resistance to them to an extreme. In 1767, Adams and his gangsters planned a special welcome for the customs commissioners coming from England to enforce the Townsend Acts. Adams intended to march the tax collectors to the Liberty Tree and face two choices: either getting torn apart by a mob or resigning. However, the mob didn't back him enough that day, and Adams had to settle for getting an unruly crowd to harass them with placards calling them "Devils, Popes and Pretenders."

But he had yet more grist for his mill. Adams bullied or beguiled a group of 100 local merchants to join what he called the Nonimportation Association—a respectable sounding front for a radical, revolutionary group that refused to accept goods from Britain. So reluctantly did the members of the Association participate, Adams had to spy on them to insure they obeyed his commands. He sent the Sons out to threaten any merchants who refused to join him.

Hoping to extend his web further out, Adams also started to writing his inflammatory "Circular Letter" to organize other colonies in the cause of insurrection. By 1768, the Sons of Liberty marched openly in the streets; the mob, as Adams' own tool, terrified the customs commissioners so much they requested English troops to protect them. The king's administration ordered soldiers overseas—which led to Adams to call for that day of prayer.

After customs officials seized and torched one of Hancock's ship for smuggling, the city broke out in a riot. A group of "sturdy boys and negroes" attacked the custom officials. Adams now openly claimed the entire countryside was just waiting to rise up in revolt. This of course was nonsense. Everyone fled when, that fall, the redcoated British army actually arrived.

The mood in Boston was tense, and of course, this was ideal for a revolutionary like Adams, who wanted to be the man that lit the powderkeg to blow up the current government. He used public occasions to keep the fight alive. In August, 1769, Adams presided over a celebration of the Stamp Act protests—complete with a procession of 100 carriages from the Liberty Tree to Dorchester and a total of 60 toasts.

Adams, drunk with power, believed his Caucus Club should have authority over everyone. In 1770, the radicals flexed their muscles out in the streets. Anyone not opposing the Townsend Acts was due a visit from the Sons, who threw them out of town or gave them a tar and feathering—a humiliating and brutal torture.

This wasn't real majority rule—it was the dictatorship of a few well organized men claiming to represent the masses. General Thomas Gage, in charge of all the English troops in the colonies, and eventually military governor of Massachusetts, called this "Democratic" despotism— and he wasn't being ironic.

Adams grew bold, and convened the legislature illegally without the governor's consent. For that particular session, the

Sons of Liberty in Petersham even picked their own candidates to the general court. The radicals, led by Hancock and Adams, wanted secession—which of course was only the will of a small minority of people, and the move failed.

THE MASSACRE

1770 was a tense year, with Adams keeping the population on edge with hatred for the English and the troops in Boston trying to keep the peace. Adams libelously served up imaginary "atrocities" for the consumption of his newspaper readers. The Sons swore to kill everyone who had anything to do with bringing the troops to Boston; someone even cut the heart out of governor Bernard's portrait hanging at Harvard College (the Sons were a clever bunch).

When in February, during a mob attack on an English informer, a boy was accidentally killed, Adams made sure the mourners' procession through the snow was one of the largest America had ever seen.

Soon after, another choice public relations opportunity fell into Adams' lap. On March 5, to use John Adams description, a "motley rabble of saucy boys, negroes, molattoes, Irish teagues and outlandish jack tarrs" nearly murdered a lone English sentry standing guard at the Boston customhouse.

(Apparently, the arguing started when a colonist offered the soldier work cleaning his outhouse.)

During the fray, partly by accident, a group of soldiers trying to rescue the beleaguered sentry opened fire on the assembled mob, killing five men and wounding others. Among the "victims" was the giant mulatto, Crispus Attucks, known to be expert with a cudgel, and other assorted riffraff Boston was probably better off without. Soon this collection of scum fit for jail would be immortalized as martyrs by the brilliant Adams.

Adams, who indirectly had incited this event with violent propaganda, saw a godsend, dubbing it rather hyperbolically the "Boston Massacre." He had a chip in his hand now, and successfully demanded governor Hutchinson move all English troops out of the city. Adams threatened Hutchinson with an uprising: "It was then," said the compassionate Adams, "I observed the Governor's knees to tremble....his face grow pale, and I enjoyed the sight."

As a newspaper "columnist," he now went to work, preparing a one-sided account of the "Massacre" read by many throughout the colony.

The soldiers involved were tried, rather unfairly, for murder. Adams even arranged for his cousin John to defend the soldiers—he wanted to make sure the defense didn't paint too black a picture of the colonists who were the real cause of the incident. John Adams successfully defended the soldiers.

At the acquittal, Judge Oliver noted he wanted to see Adams himself tried now, and felt that the radical's head would be most attractive on a spike at Tyburn gate in London.

Frustrated at the verdict, Adams commanded the Boston church bells be rung in protest. This was rather impious on Adams' part; church bells were only supposed to ring for Sunday services.

EVIL DAYS

Things now went badly for the radicals; the Boston scene was quiet, with the crown wanting reconciliation and the public sick of the constant prodding to violence. Adams was left without anything to propagandize about, although he still repeated his mantra about the English being the colonies' "implacable Enemies."

That fall, the merchants—stuck with the grim reality of having to conduct real business in the real world—were tired of Adams and his commerce-stifling antics. Their purses screaming for relief, they dumped him as their leader in the legislature. Hancock, who had been losing money while dabbling in revolution, now locked horns with his former mentor, moving the General Court back to Boston from Salem, over Adams' opposition. Now Adams worked to avenge these slights by introducing a law that would prevent all merchants from selling anything imported from England. It failed.

Scorned by the commercial crowd and losing his grip in the legislature to conservatives, disgust ate him. In 1771, the Radicals fought back and became leaders in the house again, but unfortunately for Adams, he was no longer leader of the party. He had no reason to exist—he was a man without a real cause to support.

"I am in fashion and out of fashion, as the whim goes," he said.

Of course, this didn't stop him—you can't keep a good fanatic down. In fact, this was his period of greatest agitation. Those not for him were against him, and Adams believed anyone not fighting the authorities was a coward, a hypocrite or lazy. As is often the case for those who never face violence or war firsthand, his words glorified bloodshed. He talked of offering to his "slaughtered countrymen a libation of the blood of the ruthless traitors who conspired their destruction."

His words were those of a lunatic.

Fate allowed Adams to finally crush Hutchinson. In 1772, when he discovered that Hutchinson and other royal officers and judges' salaries came from import taxes, he declared the arrangement unconstitutional. Then in 1773, Adams published a number of Hutchinson's letters—heavily and unfairly edited, of course— that made the governor look as if he was aiming for the "total destruction to the liberties of all America."

The letters had been stolen—and forwarded from England to Massachusetts by none other than that wily fox and former Bostonian, Benjamin Franklin. Publishing sections of them was unconscionable, and of course, much of what Adams claimed Hutchinson had said was ripped out of context. This act of cruel dishonesty didn't bother the Puritanical Adams. Hutchinson was now reviled by everyone in the colonies and the legislature moved for his impeachment. Adams had finished off the hated aristocrat in politics for good. (For his role, Franklin met public humiliation and lost his job as postmaster in the colonies; Andrew Oliver, distressed by the affair, died.)

THE TEA PARTY

Luck remained with Adams. On the heels of the Hutchinson scandal, another parliamentary blunder fell into his lap. Although by 1773, the parliament had repealed the Townsend Acts, it now appointed the crumbling East India Company to a monopoly on the tea trade in America and the right to use retailers of their own choice to sell it.

This was a godsend to Adams. He had made Massachusetts a powder keg with his lies and exaggerations about the British government and now he had the match to ignite it. The initial response was slow: when the Sons of Liberty staged a public protest the drew a measly 500. Although the merchants licensed to sell the tea received threats and one even had his windows broken, none of them caved in.

However late in November, *The Dartmouth*, one of the ships carrying the East India tea, landed at Boston. Crowds gathered, bells tolled, and Adams and his henchmen demanded the tea not land and the ship return to England. Hutchinson, on legal grounds, refused to obey Adams, held his ground over the next three weeks.

Then on December 16, several thousand men met at the Old South Meeting House in Boston to debate what should be done. Adams played the scene beautifully. He waited his turn, then stood and closed the meeting, saying, "This meeting can do nothing more to save the country."

War whoops broke out in the hall from men dressed as "Indians." The crowd in the meetinghouse went down to Griffin's Wharf and watched as 100 of the Indians proceeded to turn the harbor into the world's largest tea receptacle when they dumped 90,000 pounds of tea into it. The successful politician Adams was always a master at theater.

THE END BEGINS

But Boston's dictator and his cohorts had really done it this time; the English were going to react—and react hard. Hutchinson noted the mother country's administrators "had their pens in their hands" to order the seizure of Adams and his colleagues, try them, and put them to death. Although his friends feared Adams' arrest, the authorities in America were a little wary of seizing their foe just now.

Of course, had Adams tried such an act of rebellion today, he would have faced the IRS, the FBI, the state and municipal police, and God knows how many other law enforcement agencies who would have nabbed and tried him on RICO violations and dozens of other laws.

While waiting for the English response to the Tea Party, Adams became even more reckless. He even pushed for legislation to bar any importation of British goods, a measure more self punishing than anything else, and the foolish gesture failed.

The Tea Party was a great, if only temporary, success in terms of public relations; the colonies rejoiced and felt something new: a common identity. However, the gloating of Adams and the radicals was short lived. The English could no longer overlook this kind of nonsense, and in 1774, passed the Intolerable or Coercive acts. It was a blunder of epic proportion. First, General Gage took Hutchinson's place as governor as English troops again entered Boston's environs. Gage's task was to force Boston to pay for the tea. He shut the port of Boston down to starve the city into submission and hundreds of people lost their jobs. Once again, King George III was just putting ammunition into Adams' hands.

The great propagandist was indefatigable. First, he and his allies moved the capital to Salem, away from the occupied city. Then, following in the footsteps of rebels in New York and Virginia, the legislature met and pondered forming a Continental Congress.

This was treason, and was truly dangerous stuff, so the Massachusetts legislature met in secret. Much was riding on this session, so Adams locked the door to the meeting hall and pocketed the key to insure no one left until he got the vote he wanted. Even so, one member of the legislature, a spy, pretended to be sick and went straight to Gage, who sent a messenger to the meetinghouse.

The general's messenger said: "Open in the King's name!....this meeting is dissolved!"

"Stand your ground," commanded Adams, who got his "yes" vote before the assembly broke.

Not surprisingly, Adams and his cousin John were among those chosen to represent Massachusetts in the Continental Congress. Before he left, he got the Suffolk Resolves passed, laws demanding the Commonwealth form its own militia and end trade with England. This put Massachusetts in a state of open rebellion.

Wearing a new suit and wig from the Sons, Adams headed to Philadelphia. His new clothes made him a bit more presentable to the men of substance around him; his cane and sleeve buttons even had the stamp of the Sons on them. He had accepted these gifts—just as he accepted all sort sorts of favors from his supporters—not as graft, but as his due.

He was ready to declare Massachusetts a free state with or without the support of the other colonies. However, out of his element on the national level, his Boston-based demagoguery didn't work so well now. When he arrived for the convention, Adams found his fellow delegates distrusted him as a mob leader and a Puritan; they offered little support for his revolt—as well as his semi-secret desire to outlaw Catholicism .

While at the Continental Congress, he was able to employ his old tricks. He appeased those wary of his Puritanism by suggesting the meeting open with a prayer from an Episcopal minister. Later, he put the fix on the Virginian Joseph Galloway, who urged reconciliation with England. He had the Sons send Galloway a halter with an insurance policy indicating he would be dead in six days. A note said: "Hang yourself or we will do it for you."

That and a few attempts on his life made Galloway back off.

Back in Massachusetts, the government fell apart. The fruits of Adams' agitation were anarchy. The Sons took over the countryside; loyalists fled to Boston for safety. As John Adams said a few months before Lexington and Concord, "We have no council, no house, no legislature, no executive. Not a court of justice has sat since the month of September. Not a loan can be recovered, nor a trespass redressed, nor a criminal of any kind be brought to punishment."

Upon returning from congress, Adams and Hancock, however, stayed in Boston, and even held a Boston Massacre celebration in March, 1775, giving English officers front row seats.

REVOLT, INDEPENDENCE, SABBATH BREAKING

In April, at last Gage decided to both seize arms in Concord and to arrest Adams and Hancock who were hiding there. The two were waiting to leave for the Second Continental Congress. Gage said he would pardon all the rebels excepting these two exceptionally annoying gadflies. Adams was no fool, and like many a politician contemplating incarceration, made himself busy destroying "whole bundles of letters." Luck was with him, and he escaped arrest and made it to Philadelphia once again.

Of course, we all know Gage's troops started shooting at Lexington Common, signaling the beginning of the revolution. Adams had his war at last. Back at Congress, he urged his colleagues to adopt the revolutionary Suffolk Resolves.

Not content only to fight the British, he made an enemy of Hancock, by betraying the wily merchant and supporting George Washington's nomination as general of the continental army, instead of Hancock's. He continued to quietly agitate and manipulate for a complete break from England.

In 1776, Adams signed the Declaration of Independence—it was the high point in his career as king-breaker. He, more than any other man in America, had made this event happen. However, the war brought unexpected results which must have distressed his pious soul. Combat brought a breakdown in public morals.

Indeed, the congress complained of the "frequent profanation of the lord's day" in idleness and travel, as well as business. One observer said that "we are Remarkably unsettled in Religious as well as Political Principles" and "the Doctrine of Eternal Punishment for Sins is Exploded...."

Even worse, bemoaned congress, was the people were ceasing to believe in the "sacredness of private property." Indeed, Adams had gone farther than he wished; he was even running a risk of democracy, something both he and the English government both dreaded.

THE SLOW END

The long and bitter war at last ended—regrettably for Adams. He was inept as a congressman, his career there full of sound and fury, signifying nothing. He became entrenched in intrigues and political brawls; he wasted effort in feuds and in trying to control the American army. He learned an interesting lesson about himself: he was only good at destroying societies—he was clueless about building them up.

Certainly, surrounded by much more accomplished and sophisticated men from other parts of the country such as New York, Virginia, and Pennsylvania, the Ward Heeler from Boston must at times have been a bit out of his league. Burning with resentment, Adams was opposed to placing professionals or men of "liberal education" in power, as they "had very little compassion on the laity."

The end of the war and the birth of the new republic was a blur. The new American leaders who emerged saw Adams as an irresponsible old malcontent and didn't trust him—much as had the English a generation before. The activity went on around the elderly stringpuller, who felt he was too old and untalented to participate in the founding of "Empires."

The Pious Samuel Adams

When the tiny but truly democratic American revolution, Shay's Rebellion, broke out amongst the farmers of western Massachusetts in 1787, threatening to overthrow the dominant role of lawyers and bankers in governing American civilization, Adams was outraged.

Shay's Rebellion occurred when the farmers of the state, who had gone off to fight the bloody and protracted Revolution, came home to find their property confiscated by the bankers who had stayed behind making money. The veteran farmers felt entitled to free land and forgiveness of their debts; the bankers didn't agree and war broke out. This egalitarian uprising terrified the very conservative new American order—Adams included. He wanted these disenchanted veterans crushed—which they were, of course.

In 1788, Adams lost his congressional seat—the local farmers remembered his opposition to Shay's Rebellion and hated him for it. Left back in Massachusetts, he was a truly lost soul, his grip on his mind and on the state slipping steadily.

He watched his enemy Hancock become governor—much to his frustration. The wealthy, fun-loving Hancock replaced the old regime with extravagant balls and feasts—a style of "effeminacy and ridiculous manners" more suited to "Asiatics than to the hardy and sober manners of a New England public...."

Adams' career was not yet finished, however. He himself took over the seat his hated nemesis Hutchinson had once occupied years before, becoming governor of the commonwealth. In holding that seat, Adams maintained his consistent post-Revolutionary mediocrity. By the time he died in 1803, he was obscure and powerless; his noble cousin John Adams and his son, John Quincy Adams, went on to be famous, if generally inept, presidents.

Adams' bones today rest in a small cemetery in downtown Boston, and unlike his more celebrated cousins, there is no great monument or marker to acknowledge him. It seems almost a pity. He was a remarkable man; he brought off a feat no other New England scoundrel before or since has done. History can be cruel to men who outlive their purpose.

But perhaps it is not surprising that Adams has been eclipsed by Jefferson, John Adams, and of course, Washington. After all, what child would not like to pick as its parents the most elevated and illustrious men of their time? Yet in its treacherous rejection of its true parent, America affirms its lineage more than ever—for after all, the hypocritical, dishonest, and corrupt Adams is, more than any other individual, the Father of his Country. He probably expected no less.

Chapter Six

Hetty Green, New England's Greatest Cheapskate

"I thought I'd seen everything, but here was something new," said Dr. Henry Pascal after treating Hetty Green.

When old, near death and suffering from an excruciating hernia, Hetty, probably the richest woman in the world, finally yielded to her pain and stripped off her dirty ragged underwear and showed Pascal the torturous swelling on her stomach. Hetty didn't want to be there; as the cheapest woman in New England having to pay a physician for his services was almost a fate worse than death

Pascal's usual fee was all of 50 cents.

Pascal's trained eye noted her condition: it was a large, swollen rupture. She had acquired the condition over the past 20 years by lugging heavy accounting books back and forth from a bank vault to her desk. She kept the hernia in place by jamming a stick between it and her leg and underwear.

The visit ended, and Pascal asked for $1.50. She got dressed, glared at him, and wedged the stick back. "You're all alike. A bunch of robbers," she said. He asked her where she was going. "None of your business."

But it was his business; she owed him money. She rummaged for the dirtiest, most wrinkled and oldest single bills in her handbag—always tied about her waist—and threw them down and marched out, furious at having been bested. She did have the last word.

"I'll live to be 100. You can bet on that."

Hetty Green is the most bizarre of the scoundrels treated here, taking greed and stinginess to a level of fanaticism matched possibly only by the devotion of the Spanish monks of the Inquisition to rooting out heresy. Despite her vast wealth, she once spent half a night looking in her carriage for a missing two cent postage stamp.

Her family's estate, which began in Plymouth, Massachusetts in 1624 with the purchase of a black cow, would grow under Hetty to the ripe sum of $100 million by 1952. Hetty loved money above all else—to amass it, she let no scruple stand in her way—almost admirably, her greed and domineering personality also led to the destruction of her husband's and children's lives.

When someone asked Hetty's daughter, Sylvia where her brother, Ned, lived, she said: "With my mother, if you call that living." Ned hated his mother's bullying, crushing ways, which ultimately resulted in the loss of his leg.

Although she was later to claim her devotion to money was a result of her Quakerism, the causes were much more likely pathological. She indeed needed treatment as someone with a disease. One of the wealthiest individuals in the world, she went about in rags, lived in rundown flats, ate food fit for rats, and suffered a constant fear of assassination.

In short, she denied herself all enduring happiness—indeed, any fleeting pleasures, as well—to enjoy her money.

RESPECTABLE BEGINNINGS

Hetty was born in 1834, in the bustling whaler's port of New Bedford, then a wealthy city. Money was on everyone's mind: the city and it environs contain many houses facing the ocean with cupolas where expectant wives could watch for their husbands' whaling ships returning home—and bringing with them fortunes.

Hetty grew up in a the strict atmosphere of Quakerism, where everyone spoke to each other in "Thees" and "Thous" and held pleasure and luxury in contempt—at least in theory. Hetty, like the scheming and corrupt president, Richard Nixon, proved the pious soil of Quakerism grows excellent scoundrels.

Hetty was an only—as well as a strong-willed and obnoxious—child, the scion of a brawny fortune hunter, Edward Mott "Black Hawk" Robinson of Providence, and a sickly retiring mother, Abby Howland. The Howlands were a fixture in New Bedford, rich from whale oil and respectable, typical boring and conservative old money aristocrats.

Black Hawk was dull witted as a human being, but certainly had the sharp eyes of a bird of prey when it came to acquiring money; his marriage, if nothing else, was a financial success. It was not a loving union. The bellowing Black Hawk and Abby argued often, so violently they sometimes drove their daughter, not the sensitive type, to leave the family house.

The long legged tomboy Hetty took after her father, absorbing his bullying ways and passion for making money. Dirty and shabbily dressed, she often tagged along with Black Hawk, doing errands, mingling with the polyglot mix of seamen and dock workers of New Bedford. Thus Hetty learned about the fundamentals of business, but little else. She had almost no education and even her spelling was bad. Of her youth, she said, : "When I was five years old, I used to sit on my father's lap while he read the business news and the stock market reports of the day to me. When I was six, I read them myself."

She observed him once decline a free ten-cent cigar—the reason, he said, was that he usually smoked four-cent cigars and feared he might develop a liking for the more expensive ones. She said he taught her to "never to owe anyone anything, not even a kindness." The slave-driving Black Hawk's discipline could be severe—he would sometimes make Hetty be silent for 24 hours at a stretch.

The lust for wealth exhibited itself in Hetty early on. When aged eight, she opened a saving account, using the small change she got as a rewards from family members. On September 2, 1847, her wealthy Quaker grandfather, Gideon Howland, Jr. died. This was a man whose greatest moral crisis had occurred when he snuck a piano into his house, violating the Quaker ban on music. His young granddaughter Hetty wept herself to sleep after his death—not for grief about him, but rather because he hadn't left her a dime in his will.

Yet peach-complexioned and tall, with angelically blue eyes, she was an attractive girl. Used to having her own way, she made a poor student in the fancy schools she attended. Perhaps the only lesson she took with her from these days was that of self-denial. She refused to eat a meal set before her; at the next meal, she received the same plate she had rejected; this happened a third time when she caught on to what was going and decided a fourth time would be a bit too much and ate the food. She considered this the best thing that could have ever happened to her.

She was naturally graceful, and could dance and play the piano—abilities then considered key in the art of husband snagging. At Hetty's debutante party, young men came courting—the young heiress viewed them with suspicion—she was certain they just wanted her estate. She bragged later that, to save money, she had blown out the candles before the last guests had left. Such parties were useless; she ignored the young courters, preferring to talk finances with their fathers....She traveled, going to New York City to meet with relatives, then to England, where she met and danced with the Prince of Wales.

Hetty's sickly mother, Abby, who had left Black Hawk's house to live with her sister, Sylvia Ann Howland, died at last on Feb. 21, 1860, aged 51. Hetty and her father started to fight over who would get what out of Abby's estate. Father and daughter argued bitterly; eventually she took $8,000 in real estate, and he the cash.

THE HOWLAND WILL

Fortunately for Hetty, two more deaths soon followed. First, in 1865, Black Hawk died, leaving his daughter $6 million—of which less than one half of one percent went to charity. Then in a second stroke of luck, her fragile aunt, Sylvia Ann Howland, died. However, Sylvia Ann had found the pushy Hetty intolerable and had banished her from her house—and nearly from her will as well, as she tended to do to people who displeased her.

The spinster aunt had left $2 million to various Howland relatives and charity. Hetty, feeling she was the only charity or Howland worthy of her aunt's money, had pled with Sylvia Ann to give her the estate—after all, she might become a "poor neglected orphan."

Hetty showed that where there is a will, there is a way to subvert it for one's own ends. In December, 1865 Hetty, given only an annuity of $70, 000, sued the executors of Sylva Ann's estate. (Her lawyer, William Crapo, eventually had to sue Hetty himself to collect his fees. Hetty hated lawyers, although she was to spend a good chunk of her waking hours with them.)

When the "Howland Will Case" reached court, it set off a powder keg in New Bedford, rivaled later only by the sensational Lizzie Borden murder trial. The fearless Hetty produced a forged will making her the sole beneficiary of her aunt. She claimed Sylvia Ann had dictated the document to her, then signed it. Hetty's Howland cousins were furious at her for this blatant attempt to yank their share of the estate from them.

For five years the trial on the will dragged one, with the executors of the estate claiming Hetty's version of the will contained forged signatures by Sylvia Ann. Some of the best minds of the time entered the fray to decide if indeed the signature was fraudulent: Oliver Wendell Holmes, Harvard professor Louis Agassiz, and professor Benjamin Pierce. They all claimed the signatures tracings over an original. The learned Pierce even said: "The chance that Sylvia Ann Howland's signatures are genuine is one in 2,666,000,000,000,000,000,000."

Hetty's suit eventually emerged for the silly fraud it was, and the threat of perjury now loomed over her head—and jail. In terror, she went into hiding in a fourth story storeroom, for days sustained only by raw eggs and crackers .

Fearing the penitentiary and craving someone's support, on July 18, 1867, at age 33, she married Edward Henry Green—a man whose old Boston family had as much of a respectable veneer as her Mayflower one. Naturally, Green, 46, signed a prenuptial agreement protecting Hetty's estate should the flame of their love every dim.

At first, the two were effective partners in business and family; later, when he failed to heed her advice and nearly made her lose some her precious money, she banished him from her life and left him to live in semipoverty. Business was business—she always made a distinction between her money and Green's.

Soon after the sudden nuptials, the duo, fleeing controversy, moved to Manhattan, staying long enough to discover that Hetty's Howland cousins planned to bring forgery charges against her, ending the case so they could collect their money. The couple now left for England, where Hetty gave birth to her son Edward, and later to her daughter Sylvia. She breast fed them both—no doubt to save the cost of a nurse.

On November 14, 1868, the U.S. Circuit Court of the District of Massachusetts dismissed Hetty's bill of complaint; however the will remained unexecuted for another four years because of legal technicalities. Ever after, Hetty feared her Howland cousins and refused to eat any food served while visiting them because she suspected poisoning.

BACK TO AMERICA, WALL STREET

By 1873, because of the statute of limitations, Hetty could end her self-imposed exile and return to America with her family without fear of prosecution for her clumsy fraud. Hetty was probably homesick, but also no doubt she knew a financial panic was going on, and a shrewd investor with cash could make a fortune buying depressed stocks and selling them when their prices rose....The haunting call of faraway bargains lured her back, and she settled in her husband's hometown of Bellow Falls, Vermont.

Despite her fortune, Hetty's appearance was worthy of a homeless person's—a hallmark she maintained for the rest of her life. She paraded around town with dirty hands and black fingernails, wearing outdated, tatty dresses. Her life was a war for the retention of every cent she owned and the acquisition of everyone else's. She fought with the ferocity of a she-bear protecting its cubs anyone so foolish as to stand between her and her money, including her husband, local tradesmen, retailers and so on. Hetty's daughter Sylvia wore only hand-me-downs; she also had a hammer toe, which made walking difficult, but her mother did nothing about it. Ned's clothing was so flimsy he had to line it with newspapers to keep the cold out; his stockings lacked feet. This did not trouble the Quaker matron: After all, Hetty claimed, "Man was born to suffer."

When haggling over prices, she annoyed the local shop owners by handling their merchandise and often covering it with the grime on her hands. His wife's bad treatment of contractors and the town at large made husband her husband Edward's life miserable. Hetty once even bragged about a sweet deal she made to buy a horse and carriage from their owner. Said Hetty, who made compacts in the highest financial circles of Wall Street: "I went to a man who had a grudge against the owner, and I got him to tell me of every fault of the horse and rig....I succeeded in depreciating the owner's opinion of his property...."

The food at the Greens', not surprisingly, was terrible. She bought broken cookies to save on their price; finding her skirt hem dirty, she would take it to the laundry with instructions to "wash only the bottom" as she waited in her petticoats. She usually allowed her black dresses to grow so dirty they turned a shade of green—people often mistook her for a hobo.

Not content to bicker with her servants, she also harassed and argued with other peoples'. One Irish servant woman Hetty had fired asked Edward Green for her back pay, claiming she had waiting for it for a year—Hetty had accused the woman of stealing clothes, a laughable proposition given that household's wretched attire. Green paid the woman and added an extra month's salary to it.

THE FINANCIAL BARONESS

Hetty was often on the move, wheeling and dealing on Wall Street, fleeing one community for another whenever the local tax collectors got wind of her presence in their environs. While on the fly, she lived frugally, to put it politely. She even avoided registering her children in public schools, for fear that it would reveal her place of residence and force her to pay taxes. Indeed, she religiously avoided rendering unto Caesar the things that were his. By the time her neighbors started recognizing her, she knew it was time to move.

She was a formidable businesswoman—she made killings during several stock market crashes—including the 1869 panic caused by Jim Fisk's attempt to corner the gold market. She owned 8,000 pieces of real estate throughout the country.

An implacable enemy when crossed, Hetty once ruined the political career of a judge who had once dared rule against her. She bragged about it: "I drove Judge Collins off the bench; now I've driven him out of the country and before I'm through I'll drive him to his grave." She also boasted she had prevented her former lawyer, Crapo, from being governor of Massachusetts.

A woman as involved in business as much as Hetty also couldn't avoid massive litigation. "Every time a lawyer gets near me I want to throw up," she once said. Often lawyers who represented her had to hire lawyers themselves to sue her for payment of their fees. One time she appeared in court in her wretched clothes and claimed she was a poor and persecuted woman—the jury bought the lie and voted in her favor.

In 1885, Green went bankrupt; he got no assistance from Hetty, and they separated. She didn't need him anymore; she had plenty of talents of her own and a killer instinct he lacked. She said, "My husband is of no use to me at all. I wish I didn't have him."

Hetty Green, New England's Greatest Cheapskate

With a memory that had complete recall and needing only few hours of sleep a night, she was a formidable businesswoman indeed. And she was tough: she always collected every cent due her and had the fortitude to hang on to her securities during bear markets. Never hesitating to foreclose, she ruined the venerable John J. Cisco & Son bank when she pulled her money out of it and put in the Chemical National Bank. This made her famous. As she often paraded around dressed in black, the hard faced Hetty, with the jutting jaw and unyielding eyes, was called the "Witch of Wall Street. "

Sometimes, when down in spirits, she would go a bank to empty out one of her security deposit boxes and and fondle a few security certificates. Remember however, Hetty was only insanely greedy—she was not completely inhumane. Indeed, her greatest sins were against herself. She was brave and even compassionate. When an acquaintance lost his job, she ceaselessly attempted to gain him employment. Once when present at an accident, she calmly moved the crowd back and called for help for the injured victim.

She cared for her family, after her own fashion, which makes her story all the more sad. Tragedy struck at her son Ned, whom although she clothed in rags like herself, was money's only rival money for her devotion. While sledding, Ned dislocated his kneecap. With her typical self confidence and stinginess, Hetty thought she could treat the injury with tobacco leave bandages and liver pills, and didn't bother to fetch a doctor.

Ned's knee did not respond, and eventually, the injury forced him out of school. At last, Hetty took him to New York for treatment, dressed like a beggar, and presented her son as a charity case. An unsuspecting doctor took Ned to Bellevue Hospital, but when he discovered who his patient was, he told Hetty to pay up or get out. She got out.

Eventually, Ned's leg got so bad it needed amputating. Hetty, who had caused the condition, refused to pay for its removal. Fortunately for Ned, his father discovered his condition. Although nearly broke, Edward Green sold some securities and paid the best surgeon he could find $5,000 to remove the moribund leg.

Hetty had cost her son—whom she boasted she would make the richest man in the world—a leg and the chance to lead a normal life, and no sum of money could recover that.

Her fraudulent method of presenting herself as a charity case eventually led to the chairman of a medical committee publicly denouncing her.

THE MOGUL

Ned's tragedy didn't slow her down one bit. She was a shrewd investor and lender. Although some thought she was some sort of genius or magical powers, that's not true. She had a good eye for a deal. "There is no secret in fortune making," she said. "All you have to do is buy cheap and sell dear, act with thrift and shrewdness and be persistent."

Between 1885 and 1900, Hetty bought $17 million in real estate. She also invested in railroads. This enterprise led her into a business war with Collis Potter Huntington, who was creating the Southern Pacific Railroad.

Striking the moral note, she said: "The poor have no chance in this country. No wonder Anarchists and Socialists are so numerous. Some blame the rich, but all the rich are not to blame." She said the law breakers were really the "great railroad magnates." She named Huntington. "He and his railroad and the men about him have been grinding wealth out of the poor for years and years and defying the authorities."

When her son Ned became involved in the conflict, Hetty confronted Huntington. "Now you are fighting Hetty Green, the mother," she said. "Harm one hair of Ned's head and I'll put a bullet through your heart." The man fled. When Huntington died, she said: "That old devil Huntington is dead. Serves him right."

But money also often claimed her maternal instincts, and she frequently threatened to murder her rivals in business. Fearing assassination herself, she carried a revolver, claiming she needed defense against lawyers. When sleeping in a hotel, she would rig the pistol to her bed with strings, ready to blast any intruder in the night.

She had a sense of humor. During lawsuit proceedings in court, she stood behind the plaintiff, put the point of her umbrella into his back, and clicked it six times as if it was a revolver. The plaintiff, terrified, screamed, jumped, and ran to the bailiff for protection. The courtroom erupted in hooting and howls of laughter.

As with every scoundrel, she felt God was on her side. She even openly asked the Almighty to slay her enemies—in one case, it happened to be the executor of her father's will. "I prayed that the wickedness of that executor might be made manifest to New York; and after my prayer that executor was found stone dead in his bed." She neglected to mention it took months for that prayer to take effect. Indeed, she was so a brutal businesswoman the accomplished sociopath Jay Gould (see the Fisk chapter) winced at her dealings, which left him a victim more than once.

So busy was she, it became necessary for her to hire an assistant—one Wilbur K. Potter. He was ideal: he completely lacked any imagination and was single-minded in his tasks. However, he demanded $750 a month in salary. Hetty gasped. "That's more than I pay my lawyers." That was not saying much, as she usually paid her lawyers nothing. She screamed and denounced his heartlessness and offered $350.

"That's my final offer," she bluffed. "Take it or leave it!"

Potter left it.

"All right, you robber! she shouted. "You win but you're going to earn your salary."

He worked for her for the next 36 years.

Hetty's most puzzling business partner was her dog, Cutie Dewey—whom she used as the nominal owner of much of her real estate so she could avoid paying taxes on it. She even had his name emblazoned on door plates and mailboxes; she was *his* guest at the Brooklyn Hotel; she even put a card that said C.Dewey under the door buzzer. She loved the beast dearly, lavishing on him all her much repressed tenderness, kindness and humanity. Certainly, the terrier ate better than she did.

THE FAMILY DISPERSES

By remaining at the bedside of her dying husband, Edward, Hetty ensured his last days on earth would be miserable. She was no less self assured of her medical skills after son Ned's disaster than before, and thus argued with Edward's doctor, and even fired a competent nurse. She forced the hapless Edward to down squill oil, possibly making him even more sick.

Mercifully, at home in Vermont, he died on March 19, 1902. Hetty was away at the time, allowing the poor man to die in peace. After the funeral, she said to two of her advisors: "Well gentlemen, don't you think we have wasted enough time? Let's get down to business."

Her neglected children took varied courses. Ned went to Texas, living like a playboy, entering politics, and like Jim Fisk, buying a commission in the state militia. When Sylvia married, she forced the bridegroom to sign a prenuptial agreement preventing him from inheriting her mother's money. Hetty later bequeathed the man $5,000 in her will. Eventually, Sylvia metamorphosed into a broken sullen recluse.

THE LONELY END

Human decency is no guarantee of longevity, as Hetty proved. The elderly miser claimed that chewing on onions and walking kept her health up. At 72, she gladly would say, "No Howland ever died before he was 90."

But the years started taking their toll on her. In 1909, she wrote Ned: "I am so tired." In July, she said: " I want you to come back soon." Later: "They are stealing the ground from under me. I kiss you on both cheeks. Keep well, my darling son." At age 75, she got pneumonia, which she survived.

She spent her last years in New York, having run out of lawyers and facing the dreaded but inevitable federal income tax. In 1916, still dodging revenue agents, she took the first of several strokes. It happened when she was chewing out a friend's cook about his spendthrift way of using whole milk instead of skim milk. Before she was done upbraiding the villainous cook, she was stricken; thereafter, she needed a wheelchair to get about.

To ease his mother's transition from this world into the next where, no doubt she believed she would be reunited in heaven with her wealth, Ned hired nurses. He insisted they dress in street clothes. After all, nurses could cost as much as one dollar a day, and he didn't want to finish his beloved mother off with the sudden revelation money was being squandered for something as frivolous as medical care....

When later that year, she died at 81, she was buried for free in the family plot in Bellows Falls—she had been baptized as an Episcopalian for that very purpose. Virtually no one mourned her passing; indeed, the press celebrated the exit of this Lady Macbeth from the stage.

Her estate was worth some $150 million—it was possibly the least taxed fortune of all time, and almost nothing went to charity—Hetty had had the last laugh.

After her death, the immensely fat Ned sought out any man who had been treated well by his mother; after six months, he located one—and that claim proved to be false.

Not cut from his mother's cloth, the self indulgent and amiable Ned began to squander his mother's fortune, spending as much as $3 million a year on useless frivolities such as a world class pornography collection, and diamond studded chamber pots and chastity belts. He matched his mother's fanaticism for the acquisition of money with his own reckless need to waste it.

Neither the fun-loving Ned nor his reclusive, misanthropic sister Abby had children. When Ned died in 1936, ending his rather useless 67 years, Abby took over the fortune. Unlike her mother, she was willing to commit sins against the god of acquisition: she gave the family home in Bellows Fall to the town;

of course, it was so dilapidated it needed to be demolished. Abby lasted until 1951, when she joined her family in the great hereafter, aged 80.

The world had changed quite a bit since Hetty's time; avoiding taxes was no longer taken lightly, and the federal government finally took its share from the Greens. The remaining amount went to those who least needed it—the well off members of the Howland clan.

All in all, Hetty would not have approved.

Chapter Seven

James Michael Curley: Boston's Robin Hood

It happened in South Boston a half century and more ago. At night, in the open air of a political rally, candidate for mayor James Michael Curley was reciting the Lord's Prayer.

"Give us this day our daily bread and forgive us our trespassers as we forgive those who trespass against us...."

Looking over the crowd, Curley saw a thief at his car, trying to make off with his raccoon coat. He lowered his voice and said, "Get that son of a bitch, he's stealing my coat!" And without losing his sanctified stride, he went on: "...and lead us not into temptation, but deliver us from evil, Amen."

Curley later wrote, "The coat was recovered, and the culprit got the bum's rush."

It was a perfect Curley-ism, one that endeared him ever more to his constituents and helped uphold his image—only partly true—that of the "People's" mayor.

One could indeed say that Mayor Curley was like Robin Hood—he did squeeze the rich mercilessly. However unlike the Robin Hood of Hollywood legend, Curley just as often kept the loot as distributed it. And, indirectly, he stole from the poor, too. He was a good shepherd—he protected his flock from others so that he could fleece them himself. He squandered public money on a lavish house, vacations, and the sorts of toys and shows Boston's wealthy Brahmin owners enjoyed—the same people he had made a career of denouncing.

And Curley's "gifts" to the poor were not free—they were more like loans given that he expected a return on. He aided the down-and-out and the destitute, but he demanded a return on the investment—votes and loyalty and a willingness to look the other way as he robbed the till blind.

His personal charm, wit, cunning and ruthlessness aside, the durable Curley succeeded in politics for half century because he knew a fundamental rule of government, strangely absent today. The precept is simple: if you bribe people with the basic necessities—-food, clothing, shelter, and a job—they will follow you, off a cliff if need be. And disaster was actually where Curley's taxation policies were taking Boston, and his fall was not caused by his grasping, naked greed—but rather by an insult to the wrong man.

LOWLY BEGINNINGS

Unlike Joseph Kennedy, James Michael Curley, born in 1874, really did come from nothing. At age 10, his father, Michael Curley, an Irishman stronger in brawn than brains, took a dare to lift a 400-pound stone into a wagon. He succeeded—but then collapsed from the strain and died three days later.

His wife, Sarah Curley, had to scrub floors to provide for her family. Young Curley took a job in a drugstore and later, worked in real estate and insurance. From early on, he read widely, and showed a knack for organization and leadership, always making friends and acquaintances.

The power of language made him drunk. Ironically, after seeing a performance of *Richard the III*—appropriately, a political play about an evil murderer who becomes king,—he fell in love with Shakespeare. In fact, in one scene where the villainous Richard tells a woman he killed her husband to marry her, Curley interrupted the play to say, "You are a son of a bitch." Curley could—and did—quote the bard and other poets from memory— whether or not people wanted to listen to him or not.

Curley's political career began in 1898 when a local Irish politician, One-armed Peter Whalen, told him to run for the Boston Common Council, forwarding him a contribution. Curley won the election, but his opponent, the savvy old Pea-Jacket Maguire, had his henchmen tamper with the ballot boxes. Thus Curley got his first lesson in Boston's street "realpolitik." The next year, the 26 year old was ready with his own thugs, and after a violent campaign season, won.

He did the usual things a back street politician of the time was expected to do, such as shake down the contractors in his ward to provide him with a steady stream of money. But he had grander ambitions than most; he planned to be a great success. Realizing that politics was nothing more than show biz, he took speech lessons that would let him exploit his beautiful voice, and mastered a whole repertoire of stories, complete with the appropriate gestures, to inflame, sadden, or tickle his audience, depending on what he needed. He was always the best show in town, and everyone knew it.

JAIL TERM NUMBER ONE

In 1902, he moved to the state legislature, just marking time. He made real headlines the next year later when he impersonated a friend in a civil service examination. But not only did Curley pretend to be an illiterate Irish immigrant, he even cheated on the exam—making 12 duplicated blunders with a partner. When it was discovered the immigrant Curley had sat in for couldn't read the writing on an envelope, the truth came out, and Curley did a 60-day stretch in the Charles Street jail. While there, he got preferential treatment, reading, writing, exercising and taking saltwater baths every morning. Instead of showing contrition over his crime—or at least over getting caught—he took open pride in it, saying, "I did it a for a friend."

His voters, many poor outcasts, understood, and during his incarceration, they elected him an alderman, a step up from the Boston common council. Curley cut a striking figure—he was over six feet tall and was ruggedly good looking. Like Jim Fisk, he never went out looking less than immaculately dressed—and even had the vulgarity to use a diamond to hold his tie in place. As he walked, he handed out his ill-gotten gains to any poor person who asked him for money. The poor in his district liked how their political boss carried himself—he was somebody they could want to imitate.

At 32, the young man on the rise married his first wife, Mary Herlihy. No matter how much lust Curley showed for money, he controlled his libido carefully, and proved a model husband. They had a large litter of children. Despite his venality and violence, his belief in his church was a central fact in his life, and every night he went down on his knees to pray.

Politics were really rough business in those days, and Curley showed he could handle them with the best. He was good with his fists, and not above a sucker punch or knee to the groin. A 300 pound man, angry because Curley's Tammany Club had heckled his congressman brother, knocked Curley down in the Parker House bar. Curley got up, and they traded blows—the man went down under Curley's assault.

When fighting for his seat as alderman against Timothy Connolly, he crashed a Connolly rally, thugs in tow. Curley called his opponent a grafter and then proceeded to disperse the meeting, tearing down signs and banners, and even scattering Connolly's band and destroying their instruments— leaving only the hoop rods of a drum. Connolly himself took a burn on his face from a Curley man's torch.

He didn't mind subtler skullduggery, either. During one election, he had his workers tell the wives of his opponent's campaigners that their husbands' election work was a just a front for adultery. Curley was a funny rascal, too. One Boston speechmaker kept denouncing Curley, filling his speeches with, "Where is this coward Curley?" One night Curley actually showed up, and when the speaker posed his rhetorical question, Curley said, "Here I am, Tom." The audience had a good laugh at the speaker's expense.

A good amount of his career he spent fighting the Good Government Association, whom he dubbed the "Goo-Goos." Curley founded his own political organization, the Tammany Club, based on the one of the same name in New York. The club sponsored events, "Powwows," to make money. Always a dictator, it was up to Curley to decide how the cash was spent. When one member asked about the club's finances, Curley's men threw him out of their meeting hall.

But greed was always tripping Curley up, even in the beginning. Despite what his defenders may claim, not every poor man from the ghetto rising through politics need become a kleptomaniac of Curley's proportions—if nothing else, it requires too much energy. He was always stealing, or thinking of stealing.

He almost became the only American pol in history to have served not two (already a record), but three jail terms, when in Fall 1907, he was indicted for shaking down New England Telephone and Telegraph. It was an open and shut case, with the company's officials agreeing to plead guilty to paying the bribes. However, Curley was rescued by a slimy defense lawyer, Daniel Coakley (more on him later), who blackmailed the D.A. to drop the charges.

DIVIDE AND CONQUER

His key to success was simple: Curley liked to separate people with hate and pull them to himself. He got himself elected over and again by building up the divide between the impoverished Irish who slaved for a living and the prosperous Wasps who owned and ran Boston. He pictured the Brahmins as much worse than they really were; like Sam Adams, he never let mere fact stand in the way of a good campaign slogan.

His jabs were incessant. "The day of the Puritan has passed: the Anglo-Saxon is a joke...." he said. He also said Boston needed "men and mothers of men, not gabbing spinsters and dog-raising matrons in federation assembled." During World War I, when a British officer came to Curley and asked if he could recruit Bostonians of English ancestry, the reply was: "Take every damn one of them."

His attacks could be subtle and absurdly petty. While alderman, he once tried to pass a leash ordinance for bulldogs—a popular pet for the Wasp ruling class—running on Boston Common. His reasoning was that the bulldogs were driving away squirrels, which delighted children. The Common was a place of recreation and after all, Curley said, "The squirrel is a very beautiful animal."

Curley did two lackluster terms as congressman, spent more like days in jail than anything else. His real goal was to be mayor, and in 1914, the man he had to eject from office was none other than the crooked John F. Fitzgerald—"Honey Fitz"—Joe Kennedy's father in law.

While running against Fitzgerald, who had previously promised not to run for re-election that year, he was heartless. "You're an old man," Curley told the aging mayor. "Get your slippers and pipe and stretch out in your hammock and read the 'Ladies Home Journal.' " Knowing Fitzgerald was having a liaison of the sort not approved by the church, with a cigarette girl named "Toodles" Ryan, Curley came up with a nasty, but effective strategem. He announced a series of public lectures, including "Great Lovers in History: From Cleopatra to Toodles."

Fitzgerald, fearing disgrace, dropped out. A popular rhyme of the day summed it up with a certain economy: "A whiskey glass and Toodles' ass made a horse's ass out of Honey-Fitz."

The fight wasn't over, and dirty tactics were employed on both sides, as Curley alone, with only his Roxbury thugs for support, took on the collective might of the ward bosses. Whenever his opponent, Thomas J Kenny, president of the city council, spoke, carloads of Curley goons would show up and turn the air blue with obscenities, driving the women in the audience away.

At one point, he denounced an entire crowd in South Boston. "You're nothing but a bunch of doormat thieves, second story workers and milk-bottle robbers," he yelled. Someone insulted Curley and he punched the man in the jaw. "You'll hear from me if I have to break every skull in the ward." This of course, made him a hit in South Boston, where fighting is a sin only if you lose.

One hulking heckler who followed Curley around was taken care of summarily. In South Boston, Curley asked the man if he had a question to ask; the man said he did. Curley told him to remove his derby, there being ladies present. The man did so, leaving his head exposed and one of Curley's henchmen struck him there with a club and dragged him out.

"Words that had undoubtedly been put in this lout's mouth were never uttered, and I am sure that it was just as well," said Curley later, "for they would not have contributed to literature."

This election was quite a battle, much uphill. Curley planned to destroy the power of the old ward bosses—which meant now, to win, he had to take on the arrayed forces of Boston's Irish political establishment. Surprisingly, P.J. Kennedy, Joseph Kennedy's father, a powerful ward boss, sensing a sea change, threw his weight behind Curley and the election was done.

THE MAYOR

Once elected mayor, Curley shook so many hands—excepting of course, Fitzgerald's—a flap of flesh of came off his finger. At his inaugural, he first deliberately ignored Fitzgerald, a cruel and unnecessary snub, then attacked his administration in a speech. The two nearly came to blows, after which Curley started a purge of the former mayor's city hall cronies—even the ones who were competent. The new mayor's malice was always deep. Later, when Fitzgerald said something that annoyed him, Curley demoted the former mayor's brother, a policeman, from a desk job to walking a beat.

However, if it is of any consolation, Curley was at least slightly less crooked than Fitzgerald—or rather, he took only from those who could afford to pay. As one assistant city clerk of Boston said, "When Fitzgerald was mayor everybody had to pay, from the scrubwomen to the elevator man. Curley wasn't like that."

Curley craved to be the city's dictator. He destroyed the old ward boss system by giving his assistance directly to those who wanted it, speaking with 200 people a day. As the self styled "Mayor of the Poor," he did reach out to the down and out in the slums of South Boston, Scollay Square, and Roxbury successfully. He built bathhouses, beaches, hospitals, and other public works, nearly to the point of bankrupting the city. Ever the showman, he even had Catholic priests consecrate his groundbreaking ceremonies.

Of course, those who won the fat city contracts had to grease Curley's palm liberally, but certainly, at least some of the public works projects were useful. This policy backfired too. Once, a highway ramp built by one of Curley's favored contractors collapsed; he declared the cause was an "injudicious mixture of sand and cement "

Indeed, although he claimed to be the "reform" mayor, the shakedowns never stopped. Those who wanted favors would come into his office, and while Curley looked away, they would drop money into his desk. If it was a contractor, Curley would close the deal and signal by hand from his office to 44 School Street, where his henchmen would be ready to hammer out the details—the flat kickback rate was 20 percent. He justified his corruption by saying he never took money from people who didn't have it, and if he took a bribe, he would do what he promised, or return it. He didn't mind dirty hands; he once acted as middleman in the blackmail of Hollywood executives who had engaged in an orgy in Woburn.

His public works program required money, so he raised assessments on property—angering the city's businessmen. In his terms as mayor, he pulled a variety of stunts to squeeze out revenue from the hated Brahmins—including extortion. For instance, he once threatened to flood the vaults of a bank that stood over a city water main.

The man had an endless supply of tricks he used not just on political competitors, law enforcement officials, and enemies, but on visitors too. In his office, Curley kept two boxes of cigars, both identical. When he wanted to make a good impression on a visitor, he would tell his secretary to bring out the cigars. The secretary would fetch a cigar from the desk, and Curley would say, "No, no, Frank, the good ones, Frank, the good ones." The secretary then picked cigars out of the other identical box.

However, Curley's ambition ran away with him in 1915 when he moved into a lavish 21 room mansion—complete with purple shamrocks on its shutters—on the Jamaicaway. Everyone knew the house's cost was beyond his $10,000 salary as mayor. He claimed he got the money to build the house from a stock tip—but that was an idiotic lie.(Like Sam Adams, he was a notorious incompetent when it came business matters.) No, he got the money the old fashioned way—he stole it.

The house cost Curley a huge number of favors from suppliers and contractors—they knew their reward would be city contracts. The district attorney, an old Curley friend, didn't bother to prosecute the mayor. When a cry went up about the house, Curley said it was just old Wasp prejudice against the shamrocks on his shutters. Of course, today politicians can legally do any number of favors for people who offer bribes, provided the cash comes in the form of a campaign election donation...They were a more honest, if cruder, bunch in Curley's time.

Although he held high office and was in the public eye, Curley found it difficult to keep his street instincts in check. Once, when a publisher printed something about his finances he didn't like, he knocked the man down, committing the so called "Second Boston Massacre." Curley said to the press: "I hope you will not accuse me of an overwhelming conceit if I say that I defended myself creditably." Once at rally in New Bedford where he was heckled, he slapped a man in the face for wearing a Republican candidate's badge.

At home, he was a dictator. He lived luxuriously, drinking from goblets and dining on lobster, shrimp cocktails, and fancy soups. He didn't like getting a taste of the Roxbury he had grown up with. When his son Frank once greeted him with a "Hi, Dad!" Curley slapped him to the floor.

"I am your father and don't ever forget it, boy!" Curley said. "Dad" was a word the "shanty Irish" used, explained the irate patriarch. (After all, he had stolen enough for his family that they could have a better life and look down on their roots.) Curley once even ejected from his mansion the great ball player and beer guzzler Babe Ruth for saying "bullshit."

Curley treated his wife well, buying her diamonds and pearls and fine rugs, and taking her to Cuba or Florida for vacations and easing her burdens with maids, nurses and governesses. In short, he was exactly the sort of rich parasite he publicly condemned. .

DEFEAT, REELECTION, DEFEAT

In 1917, ward boss Martin Lomasney, or "Mahatma," used an old Boston trick to bring Curley down, getting two Irish candidates who weren't genuinely interested in being candidates to put their names on the ballot. The Irish vote split, Curley was out.

Curley spent time as a bank president, but he was out of his element, and he itched to be back in power. He did little of note in this hiatus, but did make one impish gesture. During the famous 1919 Boston Police Strike, he gave a small speech to the mob and then had his chauffeur drive the wrong direction up the one-way Washington Street.

In 1921, he had his chance to be king again, and it was no holds barred in this election. Curley sent out workers dressed like priests into the streets to denounce his opponent, John R. Murphy, as a Catholic apostate who had joined the Masons and abandoned his wife for a girl of 16. Other Curley workers rang doorbells and pretended to be Baptists soliciting votes for Murphy; he even paid a Klansman, the "Black Pope," to oppose him, and thus get him sympathy votes.

When someone accused Curley of being liable to steal the gold from the teeth of the poor, Curley said, "And why not, sir? I put it there in the first place."

It was the survival of the wiliest and Curley won. After beating Murphy, who was a fire commissioner, Curley sent him a toy fire truck.

During his second of four terms as mayor, he started $24 million in public projects. He raised the valuation on property while borrowing against future taxes, and kept the local newspapers in line by threatening to raise their assessment. So harsh was the taxation, businesses cut the tops off their buildings to lower the valuation on their properties. So much did Curley annoy what he called the "Brahmin overlords," the legislature passed a term limits law preventing the mayor in Boston from serving two terms in succession. He had thrown another obstacle in his own path...

So, in 1924, he ran for governor. One of his tricks this time was to have his henchmen burn Ku Klux Klan crosses out in the open when he campaigned in rural areas. This would give him a chance to stop in the middle of a speech, to denounce the Klan and say, "There it burns, the cross of hatred upon which our Lord, Jesus Christ, was crucified."

Despite these efforts, he still lost, and his opponent Alvin Fuller, went to the state house...only to have his career derailed by his connection with the Sacco-Vanzetti case (see *New England's Most Sensational Murders*). But Curley never lost his wit. One of his secret critics told him he'd make a great governor. "Very nice of you to say that, Bill," said Curley. " Do say it behind my back someday."

Indeed, he had the resilience of a rubber ball, running again and again for any office that was open. Of course, to keep solvent, it is almost certain he pocketed for personal use the campaign funds he raised.

PUSHING FOR AMBASSADOR

From 1930 through 1934, he was mayor again. He met with Italian Fascist Dictator Benito Mussolini personally, (to whom his critics compared him), and the two got along famously. Religious in the worst sense of the word, Curley presented Mussolini with a flag that declared the tyrant "Savior of Christian civilization."

In 1932, Curley, with good political instincts, sold out the doomed Al Smith, the honest Catholic presidential candidate, to support Roosevelt. The Massachusetts delegation to the Democratic convention was infuriated and refused to allow Curley to join them. He went to the convention anyway, and while appeasing a madman who thought he was Mohammed II, was observed by a delegate from Porto Rico. She liked Curley's style, and offered him the chairmanship of her delegation, although Curley didn't know what Porto Rico was (yes, that was how "Puerto Rico" was once spelled).

He accepted—no surprise there. Of course, the Massachusetts delegation was chagrined when an "Alcalde Jaime Miguel Curleo" stood up behind them and nominated Roosevelt in a hokey Spanish accent. Afterwards, Curley couldn't resist smiling at the smoldering delegates and breaking into a victory jig as he walked by them. After Roosevelt won the nomination, he made sure he was one of the first to greet the future president.

However, Roosevelt would use Curley—like Kennedy—and discard him when he was through. All Curley got for his troubles was an exhausting, expensive and extended trip to the West to deliver speeches for Roosevelt. During the excursion drunks heckled him; Curley responded by pouring ice water on them. After Roosevelt pushed the New Deal through, Boston never received its fair share of aid—Curley wanted too much of a cut of the money for himself and scared away precious federal funds.

When it came time to distribute the spoils, Curley wanted to be either Secretary of the Navy or an ambassador. He requested Italy, but Roosevelt offered him Poland, an interesting place, he claimed to the skeptical Boston rascal.

"If it is such a goddamn interesting place, why don't you resign the Presidency and take it yourself?" Curley asked. Later, people said if he had taken the job, he would have paved the Polish Corridor.

James Michael Curley: Boston's Robin Hood

THE MUSSOLINI OF MASSACHUSETTS

However, in 1930, with the death through cancer of his wife, Mary, Curley's darker angels got the better of him. (She kept him in line, once slapping him during a particularly nasty speech.) Six months after Mary's death, Curley's eldest son, James Michael, Jr. also died. Indeed, seven of Curley's nine children died in his lifetime; his witty demeanor covered a deep sadness.

When the chair of the Democratic State Committee, Frank J. Donahue, accused Curley over the radio of having embezzled funds from Al Smith's campaign, Curley stormed in on Donahue and started a brawl—on the air. When someone tried to intervene, Curley kneed the would be peacemaker in the groin and had a henchman punch the downed victim. Donahue fled the station. Foolishly, Curley appointed his crony Edmund L. Dolan treasurer of Boston— the two were intimately connected: for instance, Curley's 93-foot yacht was under Dolan's name. The new treasurer's two companies both did business with the city—one sold Boston overpriced meat and the other sold it municipal bonds.

The state Finance Committee discovered this and a few other shenanigans the two men were guilty of and started to investigate.... the jail door creaked open to welcome Dolan and his crooked patron....Dolan eventually did go to prison, and Curley was forced to pay back $42,629 to the city. Curley became wary of leaving paper trails behind him. "Never open a checking account," he once told his son.

Magically, none of these shenanigans were enough to stop Curley from successfully running for governor in 1934. Of course, there were some tricks involved, like having his workers call voters after midnight and pretend they represented his opponent to annoy them into voting for Curley.

The governor's office brought out the dictatorial, vindictive, egomaniacal worst in him—before his inauguration, he literally took a swing at his departing predecessor. He tried to run the state as if it was his own private fiefdom, with a bodyguard with him at all times and a state trooper as his caddy.

Appropriately, his bottom rested in a chair given to him by Mussolini.

In his first year in office, he spent $85,000 on taxis, cigars, trips and other frivolities. His daughter's marriage—complete with a reception where waiters served two tons of lobster—was the most extravagant ever held in Massachusetts.

But the Finance Committee was after still him still, investigating his innumerable kickbacks and shady deals. When the committee tried again to resurrect the corruption charges against Curley, he either bribed its members or fired them; he also bribed reporters to report on him favorably.

His political appointees were amazing. One doctor who had had his medical license suspended for drunk driving became medical examiner; his chauffeur took a job in public works; he fired the commissioner of corrections to make way for an ex-convict; and a felon who had done three years' hard labor for forgery was made an auditor in the Department of Agriculture. Another "excellent" appointee boasted he hadn't had a drink or lost a day's work in two decades, because, as he said, he had just finished a 20-year sentence at Dannemora prison

Up and down the state Curley charged in his limousine with the famous S-1 plates, a real menace, driving so recklessly fast he caused a number of accidents both to innocent drivers and his state police motorcycle escort. One luckless trooper died in an accident. When a motorist made an obscene gesture at him, Curley allowed his son and his chauffeur to beat up the man up. Wherever Curley went, he had his flunkey, "Up-Up" Kelly, precede him and tell audiences to rise for the governor; this once backfired when Up-Up tried to force a deaf audience to its feet.
He began to act like Caligula, the mad Roman emperor. "There is only one political party in the Commonwealth at the present time—and that is the Governor," Curley said.

He may have been going off the deep end when he began to fear that Republicans workers in state buildings would take down his portraits. He decreed his photos should all be bolted to the walls. Looking to replace with a compliant stooge an elderly judge who was going to be presiding over a trial Curley was involved in, he demanded all judges over 70 be examined for senility.

His crowning act of egoism and greed may have been his work for the creation of the Quabbin Reservoir in central Massachusetts, which consumed four towns. A thirsty Boston needed the water almost as much as Curley needed the graft. Before the job was even done, two construction companies were paid $450,000, which was more than they had even bid.

THE SLOW ROAD DOWN

Curley then went for a position of even greater power, that of senator, and lost: the public couldn't stomach him anymore. Next, a former protege, the good looking Maurice Tobin, beat him for mayor in 1936, in what Curley viewed as a beauty contest. Terrible as ever in business, in 1939 Curley allowed hustlers to bilk him of $2 million he had invested in their fraudulent Nevada gold mine.

He ran for congressman in 1942 and won through his typical tactics, this time accusing his rival of communism. His opponent was the progressive Wasp, Tom Eliot. Curley boasted he had more "Americanism" in one half of his "ahss" than in the entire "pink body of Eliot." He also claimed Eliot, as a Unitarian, believed "our Lord Jesus was a young man with whiskers who went around in his underwear."

The biggest blunder was yet to come. In 1941, an encyclopedia salesman and former felon talked Curley into becoming president of Engineers Group, Inc., a firm for helping small businesses to land government contracts. A group of contractors who paid out $24,000 to Engineers got nothing, and took the matter to court. Curley was implicated....He claimed he thought the company existed only to find minerals in Utah—that was not exactly the truth, but this was one case where he really had done nothing that bad.

In an unusual move, he was allowed to plead his case directly before a grand jury....They indicted him for mail fraud, anyway. He claimed the authorities were persecuting him for his anti-communism.

He said, "The lesson for you boys here is this: 'The spoken word is a word to the wind, and the written word is a political sin.'"

Having had to pay off previous judgements and squandered his money, he was in dire need of cash. Joseph Kennedy, finished politically himself, was in dire need to jump-start his dynasty and get his son Jack elected to something. Kennedy cut a deal ensuring Curley would vacate his congressional seat by paying off his debts and financing Curley's run for mayor, in effect purchasing the office for Jack.

In 1946, Curley was mayor again., but when his term ended after 1949, his career as politician was finished, too.

One of the darker stories about Curley are connected with his run for mayor. His troubled and heavy drinking son, Paul, abruptly died while Curley was campaigning. When told the news, he realized the swell of public sympathy the tragedy would create, and said coldly: "That takes care of the election."

But some of the funniest anecdotes about him come from this time, too. There was the famous story when Curley visited governor Paul Dever. "Governor, this young man is the son of an old and very dear friend of mine," said Curley, " now deceased. I promised him on his deathbed that I would look out for the boy. He needs a job...." Dever asked the boy's name. Curley said: "Young man, what is your name?"

Noticing new restaurant signs cropping up all over the city, Curley asked his chauffeur, "Who is this fellow 'Pizza?'" The chauffeur explained Pizza was a food, not a restaurateur. "I thought he was like Howard Johnson. I figured we might get a contribution out of him," said Curley.

To shame one of his opponents, Ralph Granara, who kept challenging him to a debate, Curley had a black air raid warden imitate Granara. He called the "warden" out of a crowd and asked him if he was Granara. "Yes boss, I is," was the reply. Granara was so angry, he claimed Curley had "cabbage ears." Curley sued.

JAILBIRD AGAIN

While still mayor, Curley fought the courts to beat his sentencing for the Engineers con. He appeared in court in a wheelchair and wearing clothing that was too big to give the appearance his health was breaking. He even had the last rights read to him. It didn't matter. A judge gave him 18 months.

Curley nevertheless successfully fended off a Republican attempt to replace him in a special election, and went off to do his time in Danbury jail in Connecticut. Because the Boston city council president was under indictment himself that year, Boston City Clerk John Hynes was sworn in to replace Curley, who still continued to receive his mayor's pay.

The time spent in Danbury was unpleasant, although the 70 year old Curley claimed he found the roaches in his cell "most companionable." The ordeal was humiliating and hard on Curley's failing health. President Harry Truman finally commuted Curley's sentence.

On his return, through bribery, he successfully staved off a plan to abolish his office; however, he was unable to prevent his interim replacement, Hynes, from making his appointment to the office of mayor permanent by getting himself elected to it. Hynes had no plans to run for the mayor's seat, but Curley snubbed him nastily the first day back from Danbury, when he said, "I have accomplished more in one day than has been done in the five months of my absence."

If only Curley had kept his mouth shut, his career would have been different. No matter. He was bad for Boston, with stifling tax polices. When Hynes beat him in the primary, Curley was unelectable, even if he was a somewhat beloved city institution.

Tragedy wasn't confined to his professional life, either. In a bizarre stroke of fate, two of his children, Mary and Leo, died the same day. It was a beaten, old Curley paralyzed with grief who stood for ten hours at the wake as mourners passed by.

His life was a steady slide down now. After one defeat, he asked about the public that had once supported him: "If they love me so much, why won't the sons of bitches vote for me?"

THE LAST HURRAH

He became a broken down ghost of himself, down at the heels and seedy. He approached promising young pols, like Thomas "Tip" O'Neill, and promised to fundraise for them on a 10% commission basis; that is, he paid the pol 10% and kept the rest for himself.

Fortunately for Curley, Edwin O'Connor's popular novel, *The Last Hurrah,* appeared, loosely based on Curley, whose character is called Frank Skeffington. It made him famous again. Curley said to the author it was a fine book. "Do you know the part I enjoyed the most?" he asked. "The part where I die." The character, Skeffington, on his deathbed, refuses to repent.

When the movie version came out with Spencer Tracy playing the Skeffington/Curley part, the real Curley filed suit for invasion of privacy. The Columbia movie studio paid him $25,000 to drop the matter. He took the money, but then brought suit again, claiming he had never received the original check. Columbia paid him another $15,000, in what Curley's biographer Jack Beatty called the mayor's "last hurrah."

Shortly before he died, he burned his papers—after doing a jail stretch at 70 he was loath to do another at 80, his son noted. He did, however, publish an unapologetic whitewashing autobiography, called, *I'd Do it Again,* an amusing piece of public relations work.

While still on the state labor commission, he ran for mayor, at age 81. It was his last campaign; out of office, he couldn't endure much longer. In 1958, when he finally took to his deathbed, the public watched closely to see the end.

To frustrate them, when people called him, Curley would pick up the phone, and say simply, "Yes, I'm still alive," and hang up. He uttered his last words in Boston City Hospital, after surgery.

It was a campaign promise: "We're going to have the floors in this goddamned hospital smoothed out."

Even as he died, his movie version persona, Skeffington, who to him was as real as his own actual shoddy self, was making people cry in theaters around Boston. His funeral was the biggest up to that time in Boston, with 1 million in attendance—only president John Fitzgerald Kennedy's exceeded it in size—his old rivals the Fitzgeralds and Kennedys had outdone him once again.

Like Fisk, at least Curley had the class to put an agreeable veneer on his crimes. Curley was best summed up by one rear admiral, who told the mayor he knew of his reputation as rogue and rascal. "I discovered later that I had been misinformed, when I found out that you were a most charming rogue and rascal."

That just about sums it. Curley may or may not have left the world a better place; but he surely left it a more amused one.

chapter eight

the intolerable Benedict Arnold

It was the most absurd scene in American military history. A short but stocky man with olive skin, a former druggist and smuggler turned general, was mounted on a large horse riding through a battlefield, drunk, musket balls flying all around him. He was throwing regiment after regiment at the enemy British lines—even though he lacked any formal command. Even sillier was that this man, Benedict Arnold, was doing a better job at winning the Battle of Saratoga than the men who held formal command.

Chasing Arnold was a Major John Armstrong, charged with telling him to desist. Arnold rode all the faster to stay ahead of Armstrong, who could not have minded that too much, no doubt realizing it was dangerous when on a battlefield to be near the headstrong general. Arnold had a long history of acting like a moving target and had been wounded frequently, as the major must have known. Finally, Armstrong gave up his fools' errand, and Arnold kept up the assault.

By the end of the day, the English army was defeated and France would enter the Revolutionary War and eventually, America would cease to be a colony. And much of this was because of a small restless man with a short temper who refused to obey orders.

Nearly everyone of note who dealt with Benedict Arnold hated him. Indeed, Connecticut will always be able to claim it produced not only the most famous American traitor of all time, but quite possibly, its most intolerable ass. Indeed, Arnold was more than just a traitor and not to acknowledge this is short-sighted. His list of vices matches any person's in this book. Arnold not only betrayed his cause, he was also greedy, a brawler, a drinker, a ruthless social climber, a spendthrift, a smuggler, an adulterer, and above all, a desperate, recklessly dangerous glory hound without compare. To ignore all his other failings seems to somehow slight the man.

A GOOD FAMILY

The future Connecticut Judas was born on January 14, 1741 in the port city of Norwich. He came from a good Rhode Island family, and was the grandson of a governor of the Ocean State. The elder Arnold was a successful businessman on his way down. He had taken to the bottle for comfort, only accelerating the family decline. Eventually, the elder Arnold was to die a debt-ridden drunk and his son Benedict became a druggist's apprentice. The profession at that time was even more full of quackery than today, and no doubt was a good breeding ground for a future confidence man.

We know little of Arnold's childhood, except that he was daring and full of mischief. He only grew to be five foot seven—like the short Napoleon, another man of limitless ambition, the military would be a place where he could compensate for his stunted size. Arnold was, however, broad-shouldered and barrel-chested and a superior athlete, unusually strong and able to tumble. He was striking, with a dark complexion, cold gray eyes and black hair. From early on in his life, he manifested a love of fighting. He tried running away twice to join the French and Indian War—although he later became a deserter. Bad tempered, he fired his pistol at a Frenchman courting his sister, driving them man out of town .

After his mother died, he started business as a druggist and bookseller. A pattern formed in Arnold's life early on, the curse of many a great man and woman—that of living beyond one's means. He contracted debts he couldn't pay. He expanded his business to become an importer.

Yet, he never learned to keep accurate accounts of his books and by 1768, six London firms were hounding him for the 1,766 pounds he owed them—at one point, he even faced debtors' prison. He repaid the debts slowly.

A second pattern formed—that of social climbing—or in his case, climbing back up. In 1767, he married Margaret Mansfield, daughter of one of New Haven's most respected merchants. She gave Arnold three sons; later, she refused to sleep with him for an entire year, as he had contracted venereal disease during a business trip to the West Indies.

He began to travel himself to buy his goods, learning to become a creditable mariner. Yet Arnold's bad temper flared up dangerously on one these trips to the Indies. Mad over an imagined insult, he challenged an English ship captain to a duel. After he shot the man in the arm and threatened to kill him, the captain sued for peace.

WAR

As things escalated between the colonies and King George of England's government, Arnold, the businessman, favored the anti-crown faction. He had little taste for regulations that cut into his profits. Rather than pay the taxes demanded by British government, on colonial goods, Arnold became a smuggler.

This left him vulnerable on one occasion. In 1766, one of his sailors, Peter Boles, threatened to turn Arnold in to the English customs officials. Arnold was so outraged he forced Boles to write out a confession and promise never to report on him; he also demanded Boles leave New Haven immediately. Stubbornly Boles stayed, so Arnold got a gang of his sailors together, grabbed Boles, gave him forty lashes, and obligingly "conducted" him out of town.

This brazen display of ruthlessness angered New Haven's leaders. Soon after, a grand jury indicted Arnold; a mob then burnt two of the grand jurors in effigy and held torchlight demonstrations

on Arnold's behalf. A jury found Arnold guilty—but the court awarded Boles the puny sum of 50 shillings in damages.
The furor over the Boles' incident didn't hurt Arnold—soon after, the town even invited him to be captain of the local militia company.

By the time the British army, in April 1775, moved to crush the colonial guerillas in Lexington and Concord, Arnold was in fighting form. The New Haven town meeting voted to start a committee to oversee keeping the peace and make sure the town stayed out of the war, but that was not to Arnold's liking. Craving a fight, the impudent 34-year-old bullied the committee to release the key to the powder house so he could arm his men.

His career as Revolutionary War soldier would be a checkered one, a mixture of stupidity, courage, brilliance, and both good and bad luck. One consistency to his character shone through constantly—his sense of righteousness. Whether as patriot or traitor, he never questioned he acted out of the best of motives. (Is this how all scoundrels really view themselves?)

This inability to examine himself soberly allowed him to make a big splash, indeed. In 1775, the Indian, Natanis, said of Arnold: "The Dark Eagle comes to claim the Wilderness. The Wilderness will yield to the Dark Eagle, but the Rock will defy him. The Dark Eagle will soar aloft to the Sun. Nations will behold him and sound his praises. Yet when he soars highest his fall is most certain. When his wings brush the sky then the arrow will pierce his heart."

Rather prophetic.

FORT TICONDEROGA

In 1774, just after war broke out in New England, an eager Arnold marched with his company north to Cambridge. He volunteered to take Fort Ticonderoga in New York. The Massachusetts authorities made him a colonel on May 10, 1775, and he headed to Vermont with a few recruits and a valet.

The Revolutionary War brought together many colorful characters who otherwise would never have met. This was the case with Arnold and another bully—the giant Vermont woodsman, Ethan Allen. Allen was head of an illegal army made up of the so called "Green Mountain Boys." After a drunken spree at the Catamount Tavern in Bennington, the Green Mountain Boys had voted Allen in as their leader. Arnold's commission from the Massachusetts Committee of Public Safety was only slightly more legitimate than was Allen's. Nevertheless, in a resplendent uniform, Arnold told the drunken Vermont bumpkins that he, not Allen, was in charge.

The Vermonters didn't like this, and started a fight, which Arnold wisely slipped away from. He later found Allen and made a deal with the giant—both of them would be in charge. The group then took off for Fort Ticonderoga on May 10. By a unique stroke of luck, the party of guerrillas managed to stumble on the fort when one of the sentries was asleep, and the attack was on. Allen demanded the defenders yield "In the name of the Great Jehovah and the Continental Congress."

Predictably, after the fort's surrender, the Green Mountain Boys held a celebration—which included a drunken orgy of plunder. Arnold, trying to pretend this was something like a dignified military action, tried to stop the roughnecks from looting. One Vermonter put his musket barrel against Arnold's chest; Arnold stared the man down and thus ended the confrontation; other men fired musket balls at him. During the operation, he quarreled with one-time tavern keeper, Colonel James Easton, a man as arrogant and surly as himself. Arnold admitted to "breaking his head" and "kicking him very heartily."

Arnold then fitted a schooner with some captured goods and left with his men; Allen decided to chase after Arnold, who shoot off a cannon blast. The Green Mountain Boys fired back with muskets; things might have gone badly had not Arnold broken out some rum and gotten the Boys drunk, making peace with them.

Arnold went on to claim most of the credit that neither he nor Allen really deserved for taking Ticonderoga—the deciding

The Intolerable Benedict Arnold

factor in that action had been English incompetence. Despite his public relations skills, Arnold was a bungler when it came to paperwork and receipts, and found the Massachusetts Legislature unwilling to pay his deliberately inflated bill for the expedition, denying his men back wages. The soldiers held Arnold prisoner until he paid them out of his own pocket.

ON TO DISASTER IN CANADA

Bad news came: his estranged wife Peggy was dead; Arnold then suffered an attack of gout.

In 1775, Arnold, boasting of his great "victory" at Ticonderoga, convinced General George Washington, now in charge of the Continental army, to let him lead an utterly foolish expedition against Quebec—a well fortified city. Boston would have been an easier target—but it did not fit with the grand ambitions of Arnold.

Arnold believed God was with him. Indeed, before leaving on the journey, he and his officers visited the shrine of George Whitefield, an English preacher, and touched "the hallowed corpsse...with great solemnity," said one chronicler.

The 1,100 man army left in September— they didn't realize just what they had gotten themselves into until one October morning they woke up covered with ice. The boats they traveled in were leaky and sank, drowning some of the men and ruining their food supplies. Entering the wilderness, they ran out of food; unable to find game, the men had to eat boiled leather, soap, hair grease— and even their pet dogs. As the snow fell, the rag tag soldiers began to freeze—as well as starve— to death on the trail. Arnold, however, remained foolishly optimistic and pressed on. Two hundred men starved; another 200 returned home.

When the now 700-man army finally reached Quebec, they were too exhausted to fight and the amazed defenders of Quebec believed this tattered mob were actually beggars. When Arnold sent an emissary demanding surrender the defenders opened fire.

165

Although the small army would be lucky to survive the winter, let alone take a heavily fortified town like Quebec, Arnold ordered a siege. Harsh winter weather set in and smallpox went through the ranks, killing off his men.

Arnold was pressed for time, as the soldiers' enlistments expired on January 1. He had to attack before the new year began. As his men started the assault on December 31, a blinding snowstorm fell. Arnold, the "American Hannibal," ever physically reckless, attacked a cannon loaded with iron and nails, taking a bullet in the leg that wound up lodging in his foot.

"Go on, God damn it lads," he urged his men. Physically tough, when the surgeon removed the ball from his foot, he declined the customary musket ball offered him to bite down on. He was out of the action.

The siege of Quebec failed. Brigadier General Richard Montgomery, who had led the other half of the assault force on Quebec, was dead. The American army finally retreated; on June 18, 1776, Arnold reached St. John's, the pursuing British cavalry actually in sight. He took his saddle from his horse, placed it in a canoe, and after shooting his mount in the head, paddled to safety.

It is worth nothing that Arnold now went from that failure to another failure, building the first American navy with the scum and refuse of the army as his mariners. After fighting the British ships to a standstill on Lake Champlain, Arnold wound up beaching the ships at Buttonmould Bay and setting them on fire. He did at least set the English back by a year.

A BAD TEMPER

Arnold spent a good amount of the war arguing with his fellow officers, who found his arrogance intolerable. He accused one of them, Moses Hazen, of negligence during the retreat from Montreal. However, during the court martial on December 2, 1776, he so annoyed the court that they ordered Hazen's charges dropped and ordered Arnold's arrest!

In February 1777, an incompetent and obstinate Congress promoted five brigadier generals junior in rank to him to major generals. This pricked his delicate vanity, and dogged by failure and resentful congressmen, Arnold resigned his commission.

He said, "The person who, void of nice feelings of honor, will tamely condescend to give up his right and retain a commission at the expense of his reputation, I hold as a disgrace to the army and unworthy of the glorious cause in which we are engaged." The resignation didn't last—he was too hungry to be in the public's eye to let a war slip past him and resumed his army career.

Arnold had his opponents. One James Brown, who hated Arnold, said: "Money is this man's god, and to get enough of it he would sacrifice his country."

Indisputably, he was brave. At one skirmish, a British soldier shot Arnold's horse out from under him. Arnold's foot caught in the stirrup, and as he tried to cut it off, the soldier said: "Surrender, you are my prisoner."

"Not yet!" said Arnold, who drew his pistol and shot the soldier point blank.

He wasn't always a success; while trying to lead one charge, his charisma failed. While riding at the enemy, he suddenly noticed he was alone. The enemy put a musket ball in his horse and jacket for his trouble.

But he was shrewd, too. In 1777, while wondering how he could rout the English forces, fate intervened when the Americans arrested a spy, Hon Yost Schuler, and condemned him to death.. Arnold, noting Hon Yost was a weak willed halfwit, took him to his lodgings and threatened to execute him—unless he went to the English camp and told the Indians with them that Arnold had a huge army. Hon Yost not only agreed, but even suggested his coat be riddled with musket balls to make the story stronger.

They let him go. Hon Yost came running out of the forest towards the English and told the their Indian allies they were in danger, pointing at the trees and claiming that Arnold had as many men as there were leaves in the forest. Between the fear that Arnold's name inspired and Hon Yost's performance, the Indians fled; Arnold took the field by default.

HIS FINEST HOUR

His bitterness and annoying personality did him in. At odds with Congress, Arnold found himself under the command of the petulant and petty Major General Horatio Gates. The two bickered so that on October 7, 1777, Arnold found himself without a command during the second battle of Saratoga, New York. As usual, temper and his sense of honor always came before the cause.

But Arnold, overcome by drink or opium or both, overheard an orderly saying the battle was lost. Arnold, pacing, restless, and encouraged by his intoxication, said, "By God, I will soon put an end to it. No man will keep me in my tent this day." Unwilling to be denied an ounce of glory, against Gates' orders, he rode into the fight, shouting, "Victory or death!"

Riding into the field, he took command of whoever would listen to him, using his considerable reputation and personal magnetism as his authority. Although the battle was already won without him, Arnold stopped at nothing in his attempt to breach the British earthworks. He certainly was spending the lives of the men whom he had commandeered freely and extravagantly. The English, too. When one English general, Simon Fraser, tried to rally his troops; Arnold rode up to sharpshooter Dan Morgan and said, "That man on the gray horse is a host in himself and most be disposed of." A few moments later, Fraser was dying of a shot in the stomach.

At great cost to the American army, Arnold smashed the British lines. His typical luck intervened, however, and before he could chase the British off the field, he took a ball in the same leg that had been wounded in Canada. His horse, fatally wounded, went down. The rebels captured the sharpshooter that had shot Arnold—a wounded German mercenary.

"Don't hurt him, boys!" commanded Arnold. "He's a fine fellow. He only did his duty." Just before soldiers carried him off in a litter, Arnold was ordered back to the rear.

He despaired so that when someone asked where he had been hit, Arnold said: "In the same leg. I wish it had been my heart." He refused to let the surgeons amputate.

Days later, the British army Arnold had bested surrendered. Although this was the one genuine victory Arnold was responsible for, the vindictive Gates, aware Arnold's recklessness nearly lost the battle, refused to give him credit for it.

But Arnold's actions gave the colonists a colorful victory—one that helped wily diplomat Benjamin Franklin convince the French to enter the war—which in turn led to England's defeat. In 1887, a monument in Saratoga was erected to Arnold, minus his name, but with his boot on it.

BESIEGED AT PHILADELPHIA

Now crippled from his wounds, his duties changed to those of administrator. If Arnold's career as general was spotty, as the military commander of Philadelphia he was a dismal failure. There, all his faults become obvious with none of his physical courage to mitigate them.

He took some time out to sample female charms. A lady's man, Arnold said of one Betty Bache: "You can't think how fond of kissing she is, and gives such old fashioned smacks. General Arnold would give a good deal to have her for a schoolmistress to teach the ladies how to kiss."

He lived extravagantly while in charge of the city. Arnold assumed command of Philadelphia, previously under English occupation. Now the former smuggler's instincts kicked in: Arnold began swindling, taking bribes to let ships break a trade embargo, and even joining a partnership to profit from the closing of the city's shops, wheeling and dealing in precious salts and nails. Bitter at the Congress that had so slighted him, he befriended Tory sympathizers; he also tried to secure a forfeited Tory estate in New York.

In 1779, the 38 year old Arnold even married Peggy Shippen, 18, a celebrated Tory beauty, and his already tainted reputation declined even further. Within weeks of the marriage, he put feelers out to the English general Sir Henry Clinton, seeking to defect for a price.

People started accusing him of misusing public property and his position. The Philadelphia executive council denounced him. However, Arnold's friend, Washington, dawdled in fixing a court martial date to try him. Arnold, hoping to clear his name, grew outraged.

Arnold gave one last hurrah for loyalty—or he may possibly have been trying for an even more desirable position from which to bargain a good deal from the English— and sought a commission in the navy. Nothing came of it. Instead, he finagled the command of West Point, a key position controlling the Hudson, and so New England and beyond.

In 1780, the court found Arnold guilty of using army wagons to move his own goods and illegally granting a pass to a trading ship. The sentence: to take a reprimand from none other than Washington himself.

This may have been the last straw for Arnold and his delicate pride. Like others, he also feared America's involvement with Catholic France would endanger Protestantism in America. In any case, Arnold began to make overtures in earnest to the English through a Tory sympathizer. He wanted 10,000 pounds to sell out, as he knew his property would be seized by the Americans. He began to sell what possessions he could, needing his assets liquid to flee to England.

TREACHERY

A good-looking, ambitious young English officer, John André, was agent in charge of Arnold's defection. For five months, Arnold fed the reckless André intelligence about the American army. On July 15, Arnold wrote to André and requested 10,000 pounds to hand West Point and its garrison over to the English. André's commander, General Clinton, thought the sum worthy of buying American's greatest hero and the key fort. He eventually paid out only 6,000 pounds—two guineas per man—for the West Point garrison.

André's foolishly dangerous plan was to meet with Arnold under the flag of truce. Clinton thought his protege was going to make his fortune by this act of treachery. Over a glass of claret, he said: "Here's to plain John André. May he return Sir John André."

Arnold and André, two men much alike in their hungry ambition and recklessness, met at King's Ferry, New York on July 21; they cut a deal. Arnold directed the English agent to return overland, giving him a pass. Things now went amiss for André. While returning in disguise from his meeting with Arnold, the nervous André met some thieving American militia, robbing any unlucky passers-by who chanced to come across their path, especially if they were Tories. The militiamen, noting that André's boots were topped in white, decided to challenge him. By ill chance for André, one of the militiamen had a stolen English soldier's coat on; André told them he was a British officer.

When the militiamen told André they were rebels and ordered him to dismount, he brought out Arnold's pass, to no avail. After making him strip so they could rob him, the thieves found in his boot the documents that would damn both him and Arnold. The game was up. The militiamen arrested André and uncovered the plot; the unlucky, bungling André faced court martial for spying.

One morning a few days later, Arnold learned of André's capture. Quick-reflexed as ever, he kissed his wife and infant good-bye, and fled West Point, fearing arrest. He boarded a small boat and headed down the Hudson under a white flag to an English ship—appropriately called the *Vulture*. The oarsmen were loyal American soldiers, ignorant their leader was defecting.

Arnold, who was armed with pistols to enforce obedience from his men if necessary, didn't want to be alone. He said, "If you will join, my lads, I will make sergeants and corporals of you all."

He got no takers. "One coat is enough for me to wear at a time," said the coxswain. This stung Arnold's delicate vanity so hard he had the rowers arrested as prisoners of war; Clinton later released them.

The consequences of the betrayal were vast. When Washington, who had arrived at West Point for an inspection just after Arnold's departure, heard the news, he said: "My God! Arnold has gone over to the British. Whom can we trust now?"

The normally icy and self important Virginian nearly wept—but he ordered Arnold's arrest, nevertheless, perhaps realizing he would have been captured along with West Point had the traitor succeeded.

When the news became public, American morale plummeted and the colonies turned to hatred for their once great champion. A mob even attacked the gravestones of Arnold's brothers, sisters and parents. To avoid punishment herself, Arnold's wife, Peggy, went into hysterics, pretending to be crazy, lying boldly, like her husband, and claimed she was ignorant of the plot. Her ruse worked, and she later joined Arnold in New York.

Things did not go so well for André. Because of his connection with the now-absent and hated Arnold, the Americans were unjustly severe with André: a court convicted and then hanged him on October 2. His courage at his execution moved those hanging him. The American Tories blamed Arnold for André's death; both American revolutionaries and loyalists alike now despised Arnold.

Needing to get in the last word, Arnold issued a proclamation justifying his treachery and urging others to join him. The English rewarded him with a brigadier generalship, but as only 28 deserters joined him, the satisfaction of holding that command must have been small.

In December, General Clinton, although suspicious of his convert, ordered him to Virginia for a vicious raiding expedition—

burning harvested crops and spreading devastation. In terrorism, Arnold at last found his true calling. No doubt it helped that he had a lot of hate and resentment to vent. So successful was the former patriot in his new vocation, Washington ordered his capture and summary execution; the command was useless—the rebels had no one who could outwit or outfight Arnold.

Both sides now completely acknowledged his skills at war. Those who believe Arnold was secretly a patriot should keep in mind what zeal he showed in attacking his former American colleagues. When Arnold returned to British-held New York in June, 1781, he was a truly feared and despised man.

Perhaps a bit nostalgic, Arnold now led an attack on his former home, where he destroyed two forts in New London, Connecticut; his marauders massacred 89 civilians. Outraged, the colonists decided to take revenge; one group of conspirators planned to sneak into New York, kidnap Arnold, and execute him, giving his much-wounded leg a military burial. As with most revenge plots, it came to nothing.

Unfortunately for Arnold, he hadn't reckoned with the contempt from the men who had bought his loyalty with their money. The English only paid Arnold 6,525 of the 10,000 pounds promised and shunned him socially. Although King George did grant Arnold an audience, it became clear he would never again be trusted with a command.

LIFE AFTER THE WAR

As we all know, the English tired of the Revolutionary War and signed a treaty. With the revolution's success, Arnold's fortune sank, and he became a ghost of his former self. He never mentioned his treachery. His pride took yet another wound when an English lord slighted him in print. He challenged the lord to a duel. After he fired his pistol at the lord, the lord refused to fire back, humiliating Arnold.

He also had that prize of prizes for military men and bureaucrats—a pension, and the government awarded him an estate in Canada, where lived from 1787 to 1791. But generally, he was more to be pitied than hated. Captain John Shackford, who had fought under Arnold in Quebec, wound up working for the former general's import-export business in New Brunswick. Shackford said "when I thought of what he had been and the despised man he then was, tears would come, and I could not help it."

There was a brief moment when he sparkled once again with his characteristic cunning and courage. When he was in Guadeloupe to buy sugar in 1794, the French fleet captured him; he claimed to be a John Anderson (André's false identity). The French, realizing they had captured Arnold, decided to hang him. Arnold, who carried treasure on him, hid it in a cask he threw overboard, bribed his guards, and escaped by rowing through shark infested waters to the British fleet. He even recovered the cask with the treasure in it.

In later years, the retired officer's legs became swollen and his health failed. He lingered on, scheming of acquiring wealth. He died on June 14, 1801, and was buried with only seven carriages in the funeral procession. Three years later, after selling everything to pay off her husband's debts, Peggy died of cancer.

Arnold's story has a Shakespearean quality—he had many similarities with that poet's creation, Coriolanus, the great Roman general who, ostracized because of envy from his countrymen, turns on Rome. No doubt Arnold would have gone farther if he had been able to rein his juvenile egoism in sufficiently—then again, that may have been the thing that propelled him to his successes.

One old Revolutionary War veteran probably summed up Arnold best thus: "A bloody fellow he was. He didn't care for nothing; he'd ride right in."

chapter nine

james "whitey" bulger, south boston's favorite son

Although she didn't know their real identities, Penny G. was very fond of her mysterious friends and neighbors, a middle-aged couple living nearby. The man, small and thin with receding white hair, certainly didn't look like a murdering, drug pushing, leg breaking, bank robbing, stool-pigeon-ing crime czar—but then again, such individuals seldom do look the part, and remember he was, so to speak, retired from his sinister profession.

Indeed, between 1995 and 1996, Penny G., a meter reader and good-natured soul who lived with her family in a small Louisiana resort town, was downright charmed by the couple. The man, in his late 60s, had a pleasant face, dressed in khakis and a straw hat, and called himself "Tom." The woman, an attractive blonde holding up well for her 40 plus years, was "Helen." They said they were from New York.

"Uncle Tom," as people started calling him, liked to play with Penny's black Labradors and feed them biscuits. He and his "wife," Aunt Helen, also loved to shop, always paying for goods with $100 bills, and they lavished gifts on Penny's children and even bought her a fridge, freezer and stove.

It was clear soon after they met that Uncle Tom was a family man. He insisted that everyone gather round the table for dinner, and told Penny not to eat while watching television. The grandfatherly uncle doted on her, and even asked Penny to teach Aunt Helen to cook her special dishes. Kind but stern, he disciplined her children more effectively than she, earning her gratitude; he even bought two of them glasses to correct their vision.

Word went out around town that Uncle Tom was a distant relative of Penny's who, abandoned when young, had made good and now come back to help the family. What no one seems to have noticed was that Uncle Tom was suspiciously nicer to these strangers than most people are even to their closest blood relatives—especially in a time when the only people who talk with credulity about "Family" loyalty are Mafiosi who have overdosed on the blood and honor baloney of *The Godfather*. He was simply too good to be true.

Nevertheless, Penny G. was taken in completely. "He was a very nice man," she said. "He treated us like family. He was kind. How could you not love him?"

There is a rather long and convincing answer to that question, which I shall get to shortly. So imagine her surprise when the FBI came calling in January, 1997 to tell her that Uncle Tom was none other than the fugitive Boston crime lord James "Whitey" Bulger, the gangster extraordinaire who had moonlighted for years as an informant. She couldn't believe it; her world went upside down. But Bulger is a master of dissembling.

Penny wasn't the only dupe fooled by Bulger's charm and lies. Indeed, also imagine the surprise among the Boston underworld when they learned Bulger, the stand up guy of stand up guys, was one of the FBI's most prized—and overrated— snitches. And think of the surprise of the federal government when it learned that instead of the FBI having " turned" Bulger to its side, Bulger had turned it.

A master actor, "Whitey," as he is called because of his once blonde hair, now truly white (whatever is left of it), has deceived whole neighborhoods. Despite his murders, drug running, extortion, and many other crimes, those in South Boston saw him—along with his brother, William, the former state Senate president—as a pillar of the community. They even felt when Whitey went on the lam in 1995 from the feds, the neighborhood went down with him.

No doubt, Bulger is an interesting man, intelligent, clever, full of contradictions—one who could order people tortured and murdered without a flinch, but who would break into tears to see a sick puppy shot in a mercy killing; an individual who likes to read *Soldier of Fortune* magazine, but has a huge I.Q. A man who came from poverty and obscurity, and, for a while, through stealth, guile, and treachery, as well as good old-fashioned honest leg breaking and murder, mastered a good amount of the New England underworld.

Also a man nobody really knows.

POOR BUT HONEST FAMILY

Bulger is, whatever else, a product of the heavily Irish South Boston, one of the most stubbornly independent villages in New England. "Southie" faces the prosperous, bustling heart of Boston on one side and ocean on the other; with their backs to the water, the residents seemingly have nowhere to retreat to. For the most part, the community, one of the poorest white ghettoes in America, is a sprawl of weathered triple-deckers and bleak box-shaped brick public housing buildings. Many of its inhabitants, suffering from chronic poverty and a high teenage pregnancy rate, have only grim prospects ahead of them.

Each year to liven up the desperate gloom, there is a raucous St. Patrick's Day parade—that at one point nearly erupted into violence when homosexuals demanded the right to march in it. Every year in the middle of the winter, members of a club called the L-Street Brownies run in and out of a freezing Dorchester Harbor. It's also a community that often sees itself, literally, as an island in a sea of enemies, a situation that worsened with forced federal desegregation of South Boston's schools in the 1970s. Little has happened since then to increase the locals' respect for established authority. When it comes to the law, there is indeed a Sicilian streak in South Boston.

Here to South Boston, nearly 70 years ago, came James J. Bulger, Jr., the oldest son and namesake of an impoverished one-armed and uneducated Irishman. Bringing up his family in the Old Harbor Village housing projects, James senior had to constantly scrabble doing odd jobs to support his family. Poor but honest, he also had a reputation as a tough street fighter no one wanted to cross—a characteristic that would surface in his notorious sons. Billy and Jimmy shared the same bedroom with their younger brother.

When it came to brawling, the elder James Bulger said ``if you can't avoid it, don't stand on ceremony.'' Young James (and his brother Billy) learned that lesson well as he grew older and acquired his own reputation as a tough guy. A few inches short of six feet and skinny, he nevertheless liked to pick fights with older, larger teenagers. When scrapping, he went into a frenzy, his bright blue eyes becoming cold and hard and his face turning into a ferocious mask. No doubt about it, he was scary.

He was also extraordinarily quick thinking and clever. From early on, James II was tough and rebellious—but he was a neat and clean rebel. He was obsessed with avoiding impurities, never smoking or drinking—he even objected to his mother spraying chemicals around the house. He made exercise a lifelong religion, becoming a "physical culturist" as his loquacious brother Billy would say. Having a strong macho streak, Jimmy encouraged others to punch his iron stomach, saying, "Oh, come on, you can hit me harder than that."

Although well behaved at home, he didn't like staying indoors: he wanted to be where the action was. "Where's Jim?" his mother (who called him Sonny) would often say. "I turn my back for a second and he's out the door. He's always out the door. Where does he go?"

He joined up with and became a bigshot in the Mercer Street gang, which existed, of course, to fight with other gangs. He also liked to be the ringleader in mischief—a pattern that would hold true for the rest of his life. He once drove a car on the tracks of the Broadway elevated train station with a blond woman next to him, waving and honking to the crowd. He became a legend in the projects.

He also loved to play impish jokes, once even coming home with an ocelot, whom he named "Lancelot." Young Bulger wanted Lancelot as a pet, but his mother protested.

"Gee, Mom, everybody's got dogs, and it's dogs and cats that are forbidden," said Jimmy. "Read the rules. Where does it say anything about ocelots?"

For a while, Jimmy dated a performer at the Old Howard, a burlesque theater in the now-demolished and much-mourned Scollay Square. The astonished reactions his mother showed when she saw postcards signed "Tiger Lil" amused Jimmy very much.

Bulger's progression to being CEO of the Boston underworld was neither rapid nor smooth. While he was serving his apprenticeship as a petty criminal, the police arrested him for larceny; not appreciating the young rebel's attitude, they beat him savagely.

His education—at least the formal and legal one of so little use to a street gangster— was spotty. Finding school dull, at one point, Bulger even took off with the Ringling Bros. Circus as a gofer. He did a stint in trade school, and immediately after graduating, joined the U.S. Air Force, leaving his brother to pick up his diploma for him.

If his family hoped the military would be a cure-all for the troubled young Bulger, they were wrong. The Air Force lifestyle didn't suit him: disliking the regimentation, he often went AWOL. In 1952, after two unhappy years, Uncle Sam finally discharged Bulger honorably.

YOUTH LOST

The next year, Bulger dove into the criminal life in earnest. He graduated from petty theft to the more daring activity of hijacking; he eventually moved into the most brazenly stupid form of theft there is: bank robbing with a gun (as opposed to doing it legally with a briefcase). Traveling with a group of reckless stick-up men, he participated in robberies in Indiana, Providence, Rhode Island, and Melrose, Massachusetts.

By 1956, he was hiding from the police, and resorted to dying that famously blonde hair as a kind of disguise. Nevertheless, while in a nightclub in that most gangster-friendly of towns, Revere, someone recognized him and the police arrested him on the spot. After a trial and conviction, a judge gave Bulger 20 years for three bank robberies. He was 26.

The effect on Bulger's family was devastating. "My father never had a good day after that," said Billy. Although locked away during what for many are the most memorable, if not always quite the best, years of life, Bulger never griped about it. Ever defiant and cocky, he never bemoaned his criminal ineptness or that of his gang or even asked for money from home.

During his 10 years behind bars, Bulger bounced through a number of federal prisons—Fort Leavenworth, Lewisburg, and Alcatraz. As is the case with almost all criminals, prison didn't increase Bulger's love of authority or law.

Young Bulger's first stop in his jail odyssey was the federal penitentiary in Atlanta, Georgia. He found things harsh and had run-ins with both guards and other prisoners. At one facility, the guards, no doubt disliking the felon's pride and independence, delighted in taking Bulger's exercise weights and tossing them into the snow. Bulger would use them anyway, although the freezing metal made his hands swell and tore his skin, leaving open sores.

"You have to score very high in the stupidity test to be a guard in this place," he told a shocked Billy, who happened to be paying him a visit. On problems with other inmates, he said: "Nothing I couldn't handle."

While seeking to get a small reduction in his sentence, he allowed himself to be a human guinea pig, and from 1956 to 1959 participated in an experiment for the CIA—dropping LSD a decade before Harvard's own Timothy Leary made it trendy.

His brother Billy, a strict Catholic in matters of drugs and sex (although a mad hedonist in the pursuit of power) urged him not to do it. Indeed, two men in the program went mad. Presumably, the only effect on the tough-minded Bulger was that he became chemically enlightened—although the experience causes him nightmares at times and gives him trouble sleeping.

In 1959, age 28, he crossed from San Francisco to the dreaded, escape-proof Alcatraz prison, a small dot in the middle of the city's bay, nicknamed "The Rock." By this time, he was a seasoned convict, and had developed a calm demeanor that would be so useful in his later career.

Other prisoners didn't think he belonged there. "He was just a nice quiet guy," said one bank robber who "did time, " as convicts say, in Alcatraz with Bulger. "A very gentle person." However, trouble refused to stop dogging him, and when he beat up a stool pigeon, the authorities classified him as "incorrigible." They were right, but for the wrong reasons....

Luckily for Bulger, he had a friend and protector there—Clarence "Choctaw Kid" Carnes, a notorious bank robber—to whom Bulger may have even owed his life, or so the legend goes. When in 1989 after the Kid died and was buried near a prison hospital in Missouri, Bulger paid to have the body relocated to the Kid's home in Oklahoma.

While slowly losing his youth year after year, he decided being physically tough wasn't enough. Although most young men in jail learn how to be tter criminals, Bulger wanted something more—he wanted to be smart in other ways, too. He read constantly and on various subjects—he delighted especially in books on World War II and military history.

The state conveniently supplied him with the tools for self-education in the arts of strategy, spying, and treachery; how to win battles and even the wars themselves. This was in effect, something on the order of a Harvard Business School master's degree for an aspiring crime lord. And when Bulger got out, he would give back to society what it had given him.

MEANWHILE, BACK IN BOSTON

For a New England gangster in the 1960s, jail was a relatively safe place to be. It is possible that Bulger's time in prison may have prevented him from becoming a victim of the Boston Irish gang war that erupted in 1961 and killed about 60 people—some of them guilty only of having the wrong associates. Certainly the thinning of the ranks made it easier for Bulger to go right to the top of the rackets when he hit the street.

The gang war started, like all wars, over something stupid—in this case, a woman—shades of the Trojan conflict. One version of the epic goes like this: George McLaughlin, one of the leaders of a gang from Charlestown, while drunk at the "Irish Riviera" of Salisbury Beach on the North Shore, made a play for the woman of a gangster working for the Winter Hill mob of Somerville, Massachusetts. Two Winter Hill hoods beat McLaughlin almost to death, rolled him up in a rug, and dropped him on the highway. Nevertheless, McLaughlin survived and told his brothers what had happened.

Then George's brother, Edward "Punchy" McLaughlin (please don't ask me where these men get their nicknames), paid a visit to James "Buddy" McLean, head of the Winter Hill mob, to get satisfaction. McLean was a large pugnacious thug, renowned for his homicides and common sense. (A brawler, he liked to stand outside the Alibi lounge and challenge all comers to fistfights, sending many away in ambulances.)

At the time, the Winter Hill mob was fairly independent from the Mafia-run "Office" association in Providence; its franchise included loan-sharking, extortion from the many waterfront businesses, and hijacking. Members also exacted tribute from the thieves stealing from the Charlestown and South Boston docks. Of course, the gang killed people—sometimes on their own, sometimes for the Patriarca-Angiulo association (see Patriarca chapter).

The Winter Hill associates were as colorful and quirkily charming as any group of thugs anywhere. There was McLean, of course, and members like Tommy Blue, who, when he planned to kill someone, would show them a $100 in the palm of one hand, and while they were distracted, reach behind his back with his other and lobotomize them with a longshoreman's hook hidden in the rear of his pants. And so on.

At any rate, the stand-up mobster McLean figured George McLaughlin had gotten what he deserved and refused to help Punchy McLaughlin's quest for vengeance. Soon after, the McLaughlin gang tried to wire McLean's car with dynamite and send him on to his reward—which no doubt would have been somewhere below rather than above—but were caught by McLean in the act and scattered.

The next day, McLean openly shot down Punchy's brother, Bernie McLaughlin, in Charlestown, near a liquor store. The worst gang war in New England in decades now erupted—and before it was over, the local underworld would change completely.

One of the principal killers in the war was Joe "Animal" or "Baron" Barboza, who was to cause so much grief to Patriarca's organization later. Barboza—who briefly converted to Judaism for marriage—and McLean were friends from state prison; the Animal became high lord executioner for the Winter Hill mob; Barboza or one of his crew even killed Punchy McLaughlin personally.

(The Animal or one of his agents put five bullets into McLaughlin, who was waiting for a bus to go to his brother George's trial for the murder of an innocent bank clerk—an incident unrelated to the gang war. Although Punchy had a gun in a paper bag, his one handedness—McLean or one of his men had shot the other one off in Dedham traffic— proved a fatal handicap in trying to draw it out fast enough.)

Eventually, the McLaughlins successfully ambushed McLean, and his heir apparent, Howard (Howie) Winter, took over—a man who was to work closely with Whitey Bulger.

Eventually, like a spider moving in for the kill, Mafia Don Raymond Patriarca intervened and helped the Winter Hill gang win, assuming control of Barboza and unleashing him on anyone who remained independent. By 1966, Patriarca, Inc. was triumphant, and the Irish gangs, almost eliminated, were absorbed more or less into his organization.

(In fact, of all the principals of the war, only George McLaughlin survived, as he was safely in jail for drunkenly gunning down that bank clerk at a christening party; he had mistakenly thought the hapless clerk was someone he had been arguing with.)

This was the unpredictable, violent world Bulger was about to enter.

BACK HOME

In 1965, at age 37, a paroled Bulger arrived home on St. Patrick's Day, nine years after his sentencing. Bulger moved in with his mother at the Old Harbor tenements, the ancestral estate, so to speak, since 1938. His brother Billy, now in the state legislature and an able dispenser of jobs, got him work as janitor in the Suffolk County Courthouse. (Whitey's job at the courthouse led to a faceoff with former South Boston clam digger and state senate president, John Powers, who was clerk of the court and refused to keep Whitey on the payroll.

"Can you imagine that man in this building?" asked Powers. "It would be like hiring a fox to guard the chicken coop." For that, Billy reputedly froze Power's salary for years.)

Whitey's youth was gone, and he had no money nor educational credentials nor a trade. Not that it mattered. Bulger, a great case for abolishing parole, apparently never had any real intention of being anything at all except a gangster. With his record, which in the underworld serves as a resume, he was fit only for a job with a crime gang.

In his favor, he had a middle-aged man's ability to accept the inevitable and make deals to survive, a convict's patience, and he was physically as tough as a barnacle-covered ship's hull. Indeed, his brutality, long honed in jail, actually made him an attractive catch to South Boston's bookies and loan sharks.

Soon, Whitey was out at the wrong places, wearing what would become his trademark sunglasses and hanging around with local hoods. Once when the police interrupted one of his street meetings with the local gangsters to frisk everyone, Bulger showed remarkable maturity. Instead of cursing like the others, he put his hands against a building and said to the cop about to pat him down, "You've got a job to do." That was not good citizenship—it was just common sense.

His credentials and ferocity paid off. By the late 1960s, he was working as enforcer for a local gang run by the criminal Killeen brothers. The leader of the gang, Donnie Killeen, held court in a bar on West Broadway, and with Whitey as his leg breaker, he kept the whole neighborhood in fear. He understood the theater involved with being a gangster, always going around with a scowl. At will, he could turn his face into an icy, unapproachable mask, dead marble eyes staring out. His great rage, which allowed him to overcome larger men in brawls, was ideal for terrifying deadbeats. One local wiseguy even said he'd rather tangle with a cobra then face Whitey.

Indeed, once when shaking down a Dedham restaurant owner over an unpaid loan, Bulger threatened not just to kill him, but to take out his eyes and cut his ears off. "It's our money," said Bulger.

By the end of the decade, however, another gang in South Boston led by the Mullins, major marijuana importers, moved against the Killeens, and several hoodlums died in the fighting. Seeing an opportunity to move up, Bulger turned against his allies (a trait he would show again and again), and joined the rival Mullins faction. Apparently, as one official said, "Donnie hadn't taken care of Whitey the way Whitey felt he should have been."

This small gang war ended in May, 1972, when Donnie Killeen got a phone call at his house in Framingham. Summoned away from his four year old son's birthday, he got into his car. A gunman appeared from nowhere, thrust a machine gun into the car window, and sprayed 15 bullets into Killeen. Police believed Bulger to be one of three men involved in the assassination. Although Bulger denied his guilt to friends, and was never charged, South Boston believed he had done it, and that was enough to grow his reputation for ruthlessness even more.

Even as Whitey started moving up the ranks in the underworld, his brother Billy was doing the same thing in the world of politics, becoming a state senator in 1970 and eventually the senate president, a job he would hold for a record decade and a half. Both men had been taught the nasty rules of the South Boston streets, and this helped them get ahead in their respective professions.

But Whitey was a double-edged sword for his brother Billy—a source of both embarrassment to the politician, and yet also of implied menace to Billy's enemies. Billy never repudiated his brother publicly, claiming Whitey was always welcome at his house and that he contacted him regularly and cared about him. He reportedly was even fond of calling him "The Reverend"—possibly because Whitey always dressed in black.

There has yet to be any clear proof the brothers ever worked in tandem. Yet, some believe Billy's official silence on Whitey was a sort of implicit consent about his brother's lifestyle.... Certainly having so powerful a brother helped enhance Whitey's reputation. As was the case with Patriarca, the locals from the neighborhood rallied around Whitey, seeing him as a pillar of the community, and helped insulate him from pesky law enforcement people and refused to say anything bad about him—even if it was true.

ENTER FLEMMI

Somewhere along the line to criminal stardom, Bulger began to associate with another freelance and lifelong gangster, loan shark Steven "The Rifleman" Flemmi of Roxbury. They were, by underworld standards, an odd couple. Relations between Irish and Italian gangsters tended to be tense in Boston, dating back to battles between the rival ethnic gangs in the 1930s. However, Bulger and Flemmi didn't let their ethnic differences stand in the way of what would prove to be a very profitable alliance for both them over the next two decades. The duo enjoyed one of the greatest cross-ethnic friendships in underworld history, on the order of that between Sicilian Charles "Lucky" Luciano and the Jewish financial whiz, Meyer Lansky.

They were well-matched in different ways. Flemmi was clever, having avoided both murder through the 1960s gang war as well as a criminal record. In 1965, one FBI agent wrote prophetically that Flemmi "appeared to be emotionally stable, and if he survives the gang war, he would be a very influential individual in the Boston criminal element."

The two men had a chemistry. He and Bulger were both disciplined, cunning, and cold. Like many other small men, they made a point of being especially tough and cruel. Flemmi came from a family that was a legend itself in the South End of Roxbury. His brother, Jimmy "The Bear" Flemmi was a strong arm man and assassin who worked for the Mafia—but enjoyed killing so much he probably should have been paying them for the joy of the work instead of the other way around.

My own father knew the reputation of James Vincent "Jimmy Bear" Flemmi's reputation as a Mafia hitman. He used to say once he picked up Jimmy Flemmi when Flemmi had a cast on one hand—the result of a recent brawl. Apparently Jimmy Flemmi had grabbed his assailant's knife by the blade and sliced his hand even as he clobbered the man with a chain in the other hand.

Wanting to even the score, The Bear needed a ride back to the bar where the man he had fought hung out. My father recalled letting Flemmi out of his car—when the men in the bar recognized Flemmi heading towards them, alone and unarmed, panic broke out and they shut the door and locked Flemmi out. Flemmi remained outside, pounding on the door with the hand in the cast, screaming to be let in.

His anger was lethal; once on coming out of jail, he visited a lady companion's house; not finding her, in a rage, he strangled her cat.

The Bear, an associate of superstar killer Joe Barboza, himself may have killed as many 30 people or more. He survived a number of assassination attempts in jail; each time he got out of the hospital, people would start dying, it was said. Understandably, the

Bear acquired many enemies. One South End native, a friend of Jimmy Flemmi, recalls he was sitting near the windows in a cafe, when Jimmy approached him with money to pay some parking tickets. The friend asked Jimmy to move away, just in case some of Jimmy's enemies might open fire at him. "They might miss you and hit me," he explained.

Incidentally, one of the brothers was a Boston police officer.

Stevie Flemmi was less brazenly murderous than his brother, but was known to be willing to kill calmly and coldly when needed. He had acquired his moniker, the Rifleman, from his stint as paratrooper in the Korean War, where he had been decorated for bravery. He was not an average low-IQ gangster: Flemmi was bright, speaking several languages and had traveled. Knowing the value of appearing legitimate, later in his career, the shrewd, baby-faced and soft-spoken Flemmi entered real estate to make it appear he made his money honestly—if real estate can be considered an honest profession.

Reasonably enough, he was not overly impressed by the Mafia and decided not to join it, as some of his friends did—like Francis "Cadillac" Salemme, who became a capo in the Patriarca family. (Both men were suspects in the attempt to blow up Barboza's lawyer; Salemme was caught and went to jail, while Flemmi hid for years until the government's witness recanted—the witness subsequently recanted that recantation.) He stayed independent—he also, unknown to his colleagues, was an informer for the FBI—which was part of the reason he never had a conviction stand against him . To stay on good terms with the Providence mob, he gave his former partner the "Cadillac" Salemme tribute money.

The Bulger-Flemmi duo fit snugly into the local underworld, each with his own crew and sphere of influence, which they wisely didn't look to expand and stir up trouble with rival gangs.

FROM EMPLOYEE TO BOSS

Before the end of the 1960s, Bulger, on the slow move up, had started hanging around the garage in Somerville where the Winter Hill mob, now the ascendant Irish gang, did business. Perhaps aware it's easier to work for an organization than fight it, he approached Howie Winter and eventually started working for him. The Winter Hill mob happened to be Patriarca underboss Gerry Angiulo's gang of choice for leg breaking and other violent odds and ends. Thus, Bulger got to meet and work with Patriarca capo Ilario Zannino, and other Mafiosi like Salemme.

It helped his rise that Bulger liked to stay low-key. When a judge ordered school bussing in South Boston in the early 1970s, violence erupted in the neighborhood. The police and the media flooded the community. Not liking bussing, but wanting to avoid additional scrutiny from the federal government, Bulger made sure the local street thugs didn't do anything inordinately out of line to worsen the situation and bring the U.S. law enforcement agents down harder than necessary.

Boston's high profile mayor Kevin White, no slouch at corruption himself, was terrified Whitey was going to kill him over his support of bussing. Sometime in 1974 or 1975, at 11 p.m., he came out of the South Boston tennis club, and realized he was alone in the realm of the dreaded Bulger brothers.

"I was never more scared in my life," said White. "I almost slept in the club, 'cause I figured if they pump me out—which, why not? Whitey would be, and they were, crazy enough to do it to me." White never played in South Boston again. Other politicians complained of similar things. Once again, Billy's official silence made the relationship seem even more conspicuous.

The ultimate key Whitey's success in the shark tank of the Boston underworld was not merely toughness or his brother: it was informing to the government. Apparently Flemmi was the first of the two to become an informant, warming up to Uncle Sam in 1965. The FBI was desperate to meet their quota of mob convictions and would do anything to get some inside information;

they even planted a fake bomb in a potential informant's car to make him "roll over" to their side and "sing." The ludicrous attempt failed, as it deserved. They now targeted a rather obscure street thug who showed some promise: Whitey Bulger.

Bulger was hesitant to follow suit behind Flemmi, but eventually went on the federal payroll in 1975. John Connolly, an Irish-American agent from South Boston, who knew both Bulger brothers, sealed the deal on a dark night on Wollaston beach when, stretching the truth a bit, he told Whitey a war was brewing between the Boston Mafia and the Winter Hill mob over control of the vending machine market. Angiulo was planning to set Bulger and Co. up by informing on them. Why not turn the same tools against the Angiulos?

"Fight fire with fire," Connolly later claimed he said to Bulger.

Whitey was sold. The duo of Flemmi and Bulger become a trio with the addition of Connolly to their criminal gang. The relationship lasted about 20 years, from 1971 to 1990. Informing proved an effective way of going from low level street crime to gangster management positions. Bulger and Flemmi took to snitching in earnest, informing on not just the Mafia, but all their criminal colleagues—including those in their own Winter Hill gang!

Informing also gave them an eerie ability to avoid arrest, because the FBI tipped them off to any move being made against them. It was as though they owned a proactive, magical get-out-of-jail-free card; their apparent immunity became a legend.

All the two wanted, allegedly, from the FBI was a "head start"—that is, warning in case an indictment ever came down. The FBI condoned almost anything their two snitches did as long as they got good information from them—and protected them to the point they were actually guilty of obstruction of justice. In fact, Flemmi once told one of his handlers about a beating he gave one of his loan shark victims that required 100 stitches. The only thing barred was to "clip" someone, or murder them, said Flemmi after his long-delayed arrest.

While the FBI often cultivates informants, it does not make a practice of catering to their careers as Connolly and his superiors did. Their handler also almost certainly inflated the value of Bulger and Flemmi's information, which made him look better in his superiors' eyes. As everyone around them was convicted, Flemmi and Bulger rose higher and higher with a startling inevitability, becoming, briefly, Boston's most powerful crime leaders by default.

Certainly, they won lots of points with the FBI when in 1978, they saved the life of an undercover agent, Nicholas Gianturco, who was buying stolen merchandise from a criminal gang as part of "Operation Lobster." Bulger and Flemmi said Gianturco was headed for assassination by some gangster associates who didn't trust him. However, knowing Bulger's cleverness, he may have either engineered the "hit" himself or the story could have been fiction.

At its height the FBI-Bulger-Flemmi relationship became absurdly cozy. To avoid observation from other underworld people, Gianturco invited the two to his suburban house to meet. He said he felt comfortable having them over and "It was not an adversarial relationship."

The lawmen and the outlaws even took to visiting each other for dinner; at one such meeting in South Boston, one agent said Billy even dropped by. So close did the federal agents become with the gangsters they began exchanging presents. Comically, Flemmi and Bulger gave Gianturco a toy truck—indicating the agent's work trying to break up the truck hijacking ring. The agents and the gangsters got along well, swapping military chatter and books. Taking the gifts was wrong, agreed one agent, but he said he didn't want to insult the two men by giving them back.

This give and take got sinister. John Morris, who ran the bureau's Boston organized crime squad in the 1970 and 1980s, accepted a total of $7,000 in loans which he never repaid from Bulger and Flemmi—and other gifts, like a case of wine.

Neither Bulger or Flemmi would have gone as far as they did without the assistance of the federal government—and many people in the law enforcement community in Boston realized this but couldn't prove it

HOW TO WIN FRIENDS AND CRUSH YOUR ENEMIES

Whitey, like his witty brother Billy, who held sway over the Massachusetts senate for 16 years, was certainly ambitious. Both men had a need to stand at the tops of their respective professions, and their careers skyrocketed and fizzled almost in a parallel track.

None of Whitey Bulger's superiors ever lasted for very long. In 1979, Howie Winter was convicted for fixing horse races—Bulger and Flemmi were characteristically overlooked because of their informer status—indeed, they may have even assisted in bringing Winter down. With no one else around, Winter gave the two his imprimatur and Bulger and Flemmi, Inc. took over the gang—and thus became the leaders of all of Boston's non-Mafia rackets—a very successful bloodless coup for the two men.

Flemmi and Bulger gave some slight assistance to the FBI in 1986 when the bureau needed informants to help them plant a bug in the Angiulo's headquarters in the North End. Soon after, The greedy and abrasive Gerry Angiulo found himself steam-rolled by federal RICO laws and given a huge sentence. When Angiulo's Mafia underboss, the late Larry Baione/Ilario Zannino (both names belonged to the same Mafioso, who was equally evil under either alias)— replaced Angiulo as the mob's proconsul in Boston, he went down, too.

Bulger and Flemmi, among other informants, had struck again. But these higher-echelon gangsters got off with just jail. A number of low level street punks who might have challenged Bulger for control of the loan shark, drug, or gaming franchises were murdered outright.

But Bulger's rise had its costs: He was now in the public eye more than ever, as much as he tried to hide from it with his dark glasses and secretive ways. For one thing, Whitey had to avoid being seen in public with his brother Billy, and generally stopped visiting his house or attending Billy's famous comedic St. Patrick's Day breakfasts. (Not that it was a great loss for Whitey: his humor wasn't Billy's. Whitey's idea of a joke was less abstract...such as pretending to try and throw a terrified screaming girl off the roof of a building....)

But the normally misanthropic and unfriendly Whitey did seem to keep a genuine soft spot for his old hometown. Forming a one man Southie beautification committee, while driving with Flemmi, he pulled his car over and beat up a drunk who had been loitering on the street. After punching the drunk in the face, kicking him, and throwing his hat in the road, Bulger got back into his car laughing and drove off. A state trooper who had been tailing the pair approached the wino, who pushed him away.

"I don't know nothin'" said the drunk. "And leave me alone." As usual, a magical silence followed Whitey wherever he went....

He was a local to the end. People from the neighborhood lined up to see him, looking for advice and favors, as if he was some sort of Godfather. He liked to sun himself outside the South Boston liquor store (at gun-point, Whitey and Flemmi had coerced the original owner to sell it).

When in his native South Boston, the cold, harsh front fell away, replaced by a pleasant, harmless dishonest one. He smiled, greeted children, helped old women cross the street or carry their grocery bags up to their apartments. He gave money to homeless men— so the story goes—and to wives with husbands in jail. At Christmas, Bulger gave out turkeys and baskets.

As there was no real beginning to Bulger's benevolence, so was there no real end. Once, a story has it, a boy lost his dog in a car accident. The next day, Whitey was at the boy's house with a puppy. Noblesse oblige or just good public relations? Truth or Whitey propaganda? Probably a bit of both.

After all, a street crook like Bulger depends on the locals to shield him from the law. They tip him off to strangers in the neighborhood who might really be snooping law enforcement agents, and generally refuse to cooperate with the police. South

Boston never caught on to Whitey. Residents didn't say much of anything about Bulger—or his brother, for that matter—unless it was good. It wasn't exactly love. People who shot their mouths off got beaten; if they kept being foolish, they knew they might vanish.

As one prosecutor observed, "Everybody's scared to death of him."

And of course, people like to mythologize their local gangsters as pillars of society, as the Providence Italians did with Raymond Patriarca. The residents were sold on the idea Bulger was doing the community a service, that it was a kind of privilege that he allowed them to live in his town. People believed he kept the worst of the street rats in line and kept drugs out. These propositions were false. The truth was, he employed the worst street rats for his own uses and kept out only the drugs he wasn't profiting on. Indeed, law enforcement personnel believed Bulger ran a rather lucrative Miami to Boston drug importing business....

According to one yarn, some Vietnamese youths peddling drugs in Southie received a beating at Bulger's command, after a complaint from a South Boston mother. This rings about as true as a pre-election campaign promise from a politician—it sounds like Bulger's own fiction. But if true, it only proved any drug dealer in Bulger's territory needed Bulger's imprimatur to ply his craft. The extortion was lucrative—dealers allegedly paid Bulger and company millions over the years.

Bulger, who said, "Drug dealers would sell their mothers," may have personally disliked the profession, but he dealt with them, and shook them down when they didn't pay.

KINGS OF THE CITY

By the end of 1980, the Bulger-Flemmi duo had made an uneasy alliance with the Mafia they were informing on. Working out of a North Station garage, they met their criminal appointments out in the street and then took them inside to do business. They were always neatly dressed, and although in their 50s, they were ready to stare down and frighten passers-by as if they were punks 20 years younger. Gangsters went in and out of the garage, carrying briefcases stuffed with cash, cutting deals and paying their tithes with religious faithfulness.

The two men had become a force to be reckoned with. Bulger and Flemmi's takeover of the Winter Hill mob was a success. Though shaken up, the gang was still intact, and the FBI was willing to overlook its more nefarious activities because of its leaders' snitch status.

From 1980 on, the DEA and the Massachusetts state police went all out trying to catch the notorious Bulger. They tried to penetrate the North Station garage again and again unsuccessfully. Over and over they tried to plant a bug in his car, home or telephone, to no avail. Or when they did succeed, Bulger always had an eerie foresight to stop talking. What the agents didn't realize was a bug was less than useless. It was redundant. If they wanted Whitey to talk, all they needed to do was change agencies.

In the meantime, Junior Patriarca (Raymond Senior's heir), Angiulo, Howie Winter, and others went down, one right after the other, often with a nudge from the Bulger/Flemmi team.

But they took no chances. To prevent bugging, Bulger and Flemmi often held outdoor meetings in crowded places like Castle Island in South Boston, where high-technology surveillance tools were useless. When Bulger had to drive, he would lease a car. He avoided photographers and publicity to the point where the public didn't even know what he looked like.

If he had incriminating documents, he would burn them or tear them up in his apartments—much to the chagrin of the police picking through his garbage for evidence. He made phone calls from public booths; bystanders often saw him fishing for dimes in his pocket. When a bank of phones in Dorchester he often used got tapped, the FBI tipped Whitey off about it. The very day the tap took effect, Bulger stopped using the phones. No one could predict what he was up to—he worked nights and never fell into a routine.

Bulger also discouraged other kinds of snoops—such as the press. When Bulger shot a bookmaker-turned-drug dealer in the head at a bar in 1980, a *Boston Herald* reporter began asking questions about the incident. Full of answers, Bulger confronted the reporter at a downtown bar, and threatened him, those famous steel eyes glaring out icily.

"Well, my name is Whitey Bulger, motherfucker, and I kill people for a living," he said.

He also told the reporter he knew where the reporter lived and where his daughter attended kindergarten. The reporter, terrified, told the Boston police, who in turn confronted Bulger. The crime boss admitted he had been naughty: "I lost my temper," he said.

The continuing relationship with the FBI got bizarre. It is virtually a miracle that cars from different agencies tailing Bulger and Flemmi never collided with one another, there was so much overlap.

And, at times, it wasn't clear who was stalking whom. Flemmi and Bulger actually peered through binoculars at the undercover agents watching them and wrote their license plate numbers down for future reference or monitored police radios for information.

The two were vigilant. One night, around midnight, Connolly visited Bulger at the gangster's Quincy condominium (Bulger wasn't totally tied to his home town). Bulger noted that a car in the parking lot belonged to state trooper Jack O'Donovan, an "honest cop" who had a "continuing vendetta" against Bulger for a failed 1980 bugging attempt at the Lancaster Street garage.

The fighting went from the streets to the state house. A small coalition formed in the Massachusetts Legislature to fight back against the Bulger brothers; they egged the state police on to nail Whitey. Seeing this, someone, (presumably Billy Bulger or one of his political henchmen) tried passing legislation sending two state troopers—i.e., the ones who had planted the garage bug—into retirement. While no one was sure just who had inserted the language, it was obvious Billy Bulger was reaching out to help his older brother.

But it got worse than that. Indeed, the relationship between the government and the Winter Hill mob may have proved lethal for would-be government informant Edward Halloran. A coke dealer and murderer, Halloran had been approached by John Callahan, one time president of World Jai Alai in Connecticut, and told him he needed Halloran to kill a Tulsa businessman who wanted to get rid of organized crime at World Jai Alai. It just so happened, the organized crime element meant Flemmi and Bulger and the Winter Hill mob, who had "a piece of the action" with a skimming operation there.

Callahan offered Halloran a $20,000 murder contract, but two weeks later told him he was not needed to do the hit, but let him keep the cash as hush money.

In May, 1981, said informants, Bulger, Flemmi and a triggerman gunned down the millionaire businessman outside of a Tulsa country club. Then, apparently, the Bulger-Flemmi duo decided they needed to remove Halloran from the picture, as well. After gunmen opened fire on Halloran outside his Quincy apartment, and he saw Bulger and Flemmi tailing him in a van, Halloran decided it was time to go to the FBI and, without knowing it, play their own game, informing against them.

However, Morris, the head of the FBI organized crime squad, wound up telling the pair's handler, special agent Connolly. With his usual thoroughness and zeal for justice, Connolly asked them if they had any part of Wheeler's murder. They denied it....Big surprise....

On May, 11, 1982, Halloran and an unfortunate friend left a waterfront Boston bar to be greeted by a hail of gunfire that killed them both. Several months later, Callahan's body surfaced in the trunk in the Miami airport.

Morris later said he feared he might have caused the drug dealer's murder. Bulger and Flemmi denied killing any of the Jai Alai trio, but of course they have denied virtually every crime they committed, and in this case refused to take a polygraph.

Whitey, something of an IRA sympathizer, put money up in 1983 to run guns and ammunition to Ireland. After the ship, the

Valhalla, left for his parents' homeland, Bulger tipped off the authorities, possibly putting him on the IRA death list. Law enforcement agents who had planted a microphone in Bulger's Quincy condominium heard him say, "That's our stuff" when he saw the announcement about the boat's seizure on television.

Indeed, one of the crew members, John McIntyre, was also informing authorities about the boat—a very leaky vessel, one might say—and it appears Bulger and Flemmi tortured and killed him for it. After all, they had their own gunrunning operation to protect.

THE HUNT CONTINUES

Connolly noted in one report Bulger knew he was being followed and suspected the Quincy police had bugged his home while patrolmen were answering an alarm that went off there. Connolly wrote: "Both sources are not overly concerned about the increased attention and used terms like 'window of vulnerability' to describe the precautions they take to routinely survive. Both read extensively on current state-of-the art electronic eavesdropping equipment and do not talk business on phones, in cars, in rooms or offices of any kinds, anywhere."

They remained in a state of alert round the clock, never talking to strangers, and always checking anyone approaching them for weapons. They went so far as to put pressure plates in their cars and houses to detect any intruders and spent $12,000 in debugging equipment. But the farce went on and on as the non-FBI law enforcement agencies kept after the duo.

Indeed, the state police stopped Flemmi in 1982 on Blue Hill Avenue in Roxbury and planted a bug in his car. Flemmi found the bug, and sold the car—without bothering to remove the bug, saying "They must think that we just fell off the turnip truck."

In 1983, DEA agents raided a warehouse in South Boston, found $6 million worth of marijuana they knew was connected to Bulger, but were unable to do so much as to lift a fingerprint from him. In 1984, the DEA wound up looking silly when Bulger discovered or was tipped off to a bug in his car, after which he took the car to a garage. Fearing they would lose $50,000 in equipment, the DEA went into the garage, identified themselves and removed the surveillance equipment themselves.

"We're all good guys here," said Bulger. "You're the good-good guys, and were the bad-good guys." Soon after, Bulger flagged the DEA agents down in the street, and said he was surprised they hadn't triggered the alarm in his car when they had planted the bug.

Despite such a setback, the DEA didn't give up, and not known for great brainpower, even drilled a hole in the wall in Bulger's Quincy condominium and put a listening device there. It didn't work. Every time Flemmi started to speak, Bulger snapped his finger and said, "Hey, be quiet."

The state police organized crime unit was so stymied in their attempts to get through to the blessed duo, they even began calling themselves the "Losers." To pass the time, as they watched the hoodlums go in and out of Bulger's headquarters, they killed cockroaches, noting their size and time of death.

One man crept into the garage headquarters by hiding under the floor of a van; the bug he planted inside didn't work. Another bug placed under a couch was crushed when a 400-pound gangster sat on it.

When the bugs worked, they worked badly, picking up random transmissions from all over the city, or television broadcasts. At one point, when in the North End, Bulger and Flemmi who had been conversing openly, suddenly stopped and got in a car so they couldn't be overheard. When the conversations were audible, they were revealing—about anything except crime. The duo would say things like, "You can't walk the streets anymore...it's terrible how bad the crime is."

The state agents did hear Bulger denounce the television cop show, "The Rookies," as it depicted the Irish police as fools. They knew they were being had when they heard one gangster warning another to drive carefully when going on vacation, as the state police were very diligent.

The state troopers, however, did seem to get one piece of good luck when in 1983 they managed to plant a bug in the mob run Chelsea bar, Heller's. They learned much about who was paying rent to the Mafia and the Winter Hill gang. It was the beginning of a case against Bulger. However, this operation would not bear fruit for another decade....

In the meantime, Bulger went on unmolested, accumulating a fortune of perhaps $25 million. It is not surprising he seemed to good-naturedly indulge the police in their buffoonish attempts to capture him—he could afford to. However, when once he caught the lawmen trying to secrete a bug in his car and mistakenly thought they were planting a bomb, he exploded in one of his signature fits of rage. He started screaming at them and chased them to a police "safe" house where he issued them a warning not to trifle with Whitey Bulger.

After all, he was a kind of royalty.

ON TOP

The two men became powerful—anyone in the underworld in the kingdom of Boston's two criminal Caesars had to pay tribute, or "rent," to prevent harassment and worse. One area bookie was overheard telling an associate the extortion money "pays for itself in one year."

The two also crossed ethnic lines in a city whose underworld was traditionally defined by tribe. Bulger and Flemmi worked with Jews based in Newton and Brookline.

By the early 1980s, Gerry Angiulo would say: "Whitey's got the whole of Southie. Stevie is got the whole of the South End."

The Winter Hill gang took Angiulo's surplus money and put it out in the street in the form of illegally high interest loans. The gang paid one-to-two percent interest a week on the money, and lent it out at five or six percent. Anyone wanting to operate in Bulger or Flemmi's territories needed their permission to do so. Both the Angiulos and their lieutenant, Larry Zannino, loved

Bulger and his crew. Gerry Angiulo once said, "I'll tell you right now, if I called these guys right now they'd kill anybody we tell 'em to."

Bulger had become prosperous, doing freelance murders and other jobs for the Mafia. "Don't say you're broke," said Angiulo to Bulger. " I know 50 guys that claim they give you $1,000 a month, $400 a week, $300 a week. That's $50,000 a month."

However, the penny-pinching Angiulo lamented a debt of $245,000 the pair owed him. "When did they ever come down here and give me a quarter?" asked Angiulo. "And I'll tell you something, I don't think they intend to pay it, if you want my honest opinion."

The old fashioned, red blooded, leg breaking Mafioso Zannino echoed those sentiments "These are nice people. These are the kind of fucking people that straighten a thing out." Another time, however, the moody Zannino was ready to take a machine gun to his proteges. "We'll kill every one of these Irishmen," he said.

By informing on him, Bulger got to Zannino first.

However, Zannino, unlike the FBI, did once at least wonder just who Bulger and Flemmi really worked for. Early one morning, he warned an associate of his not to welsh on an $80,000 debt to the duo, because, as he drunkenly explained, the Winter Hill boys were on the Mafia's side—sort of. Then, in a moment of reality, he asked an underling: "Are they with us? Are they with us?"

Bulger liked having both fixed and mobile headquarters. He had residences in South Boston and in Quincy. He acquired a liquor store in South Boston by forcing its owner to sell it to one of his punks—with a veiled threat that if the owner didn't sell, Flemmi would kill his child.

The two had gone to see the owner, whose child was present during the meeting. Flemmi took out a gun and set it down in front of the liquor store owner.

"It would be a shame not to see your children grow up," said Bulger. When the owner told the Boston police, the police told the FBI, who told Connolly, who told Bulger, who told the owner silence was golden.

After acquiring the establishment, Bulger imaginatively renamed it the South Boston Liquor Mart, in whose bathroom authorities believed "something big" was going on—or so a businessman who owed Bulger a favor told the kingpin, warning him that a drunken Quincy detective had blurted out to him a bug was going to be placed there.

(This story is worth mentioning. The businessman who had told Bulger about the detective's remarks had a daughter with a black boyfriend, a former boxer (why do so many people who get involved with the underworld have a connection to boxing?) and weightlifter who was pimping for a living. The daughter wanted to end the relationship, but the pimp had grown too attached to her. Bulger showed the man the light of reason and convinced him, somehow, to drop the woman. Bulger himself claimed to have "coaxed' this gentleman to agree to break off the relationship, no doubt appealing to his reason and his innate goodness. The Quincy detective also leaked the fact he knew Bulger had drug connections in Montreal. Bulger denied it to the FBI. Nevertheless, Bulger was caught later at Logan Airport—with a bag full of something like $100,000— heading to Montreal—it was unlikely this was charity money.)

But Bulger also moved his operation all around the city— from a set of public phones in Dorchester to his car to a smoke shop behind Boston city hall from where he could walk over and visit Donato Angiulo in the Cafe Pompeii, the center of Boston Mafia's loanshark business.

His lifestyle, like that of so many career gangsters, was rather low key. (What do they spend their money on if they don't gamble?) For a while, on the weekends, he'd indulge himself by tooling around in a Cadillac or a Jaguar; sometimes he'd take a Caribbean vacation, but nothing too lavish. Becoming a gentleman, he even tried his hand at sailing.

He remained low key, almost invisible. He could blend into the endless three deckers of South Boston easily—in fact, no one was sure just where Bulger lived. In the years between prison and flight, he went to court only twice, for traffic violations. He kept his belongings under his girlfriend's name— like his car, a blue Ford LTD, the sort favored by police and elderly men.

Bulger became a fashion plait for the local mob, appearing in casual athletic clothes, showing off his physique even in his 60s, no doubt trying to make up for the youth jail had cheated him of— and no doubt had he not been a gangster, would have looked completely foolish.

Like Joseph Kennedy, Bulger was a retailer of liquors who didn't drink, and didn't trust those who did, as they "were weak" and might inform on him. Public intoxication at the St. Patrick's day parade in his hometown irked him.

When it came to sex, he was a little less uptight. His puritanical brother may have winced, but Whitey had two girlfriends—Theresa Stanley, who was his regular companion in South Boston, and Catherine Greig, of Quincy—later to be "Aunt Helen." Stanley was a mother with grown children; Greig, a dog groomer and dental hygienist, about 20 years younger. Bulger shared some of his life—lives— with both women; with his gift for deceit, he kept Stanley from finding out about Greig. Stanley later said of Bulger that he was good with disciplining her children, but was bitter about his deception. He shut her out of his private life completely.

Bulger's romantic life had its discords, however. "You care more about the fucking dogs than you do about me," he once screamed at Greig.

A DEAL WITH THE DEVIL

At its height, the Bulger-Flemmi empire covered South Boston, Roxbury, Jamaica Plain, the South End, Quincy, and Lowell and Brockton. The Bulger-Flemmi concern offered a wide portfolio of illegalities, embracing gaming, loan-sharking, money-laundering, cocaine and illicit liquor sales, Mafia assassinations, marijuana smuggling, theft, and anything else that happened to cross their paths.

Their biggest break came when Angiulo and 40 relatives and employees were arrested and tried in 1986. The FBI overheard Angiulo say, among other things: "We're a shylock. We're a fucking bookmaker. We're selling marijuana....We're illegal here, illegal there. Arsonists! Every fucking thing."

As the Patriarca consigliere Henry "Referee" Tameleo, said: "Mr. Patriarca gave 'em the rope that they used. They never did anything right."

With Angiulo and company safely tucked away in jail, Bulger and Flemmi became the CEOs of the Boston crime world. With Bulger's ascendancy, the Irish mob now had its day again. The Mafia had been the ascendant criminal organization since Prohibition, when the North End-based Italian bootleggers led by Joe Lombardo gunned down and eventually superceded their Irish rivals. With Bulger, and Flemmi, an unofficial "Irish" gangster, working with mostly Irish FBI agents, it was the turn of the Italian Mafia to go down.

Remarkably, no one ever made much of the fact that the president of the state Senate—the most powerful man in the Commonwealth's government—had a brother who was president of the state's underworld. Politicians believed bringing up the relationship was political—and possibly literal—suicide.

"It's exactly as if Al Capone's brother was president of the Illinois state senate," said a former state senate president, "and nobody ever mentioned it."

Despite Whitey's public reputation—a 1986 presidential commission on crime labeled him as a major crime boss—which made him express his ire to friends at a wedding reception—the deal with Connolly went on and on. In 1988, the two were warned to avoid associating with a bookmaker, John Baharoian, who was about to be bugged and have his phone tapped.

He didn't object to a little old fashioned extortion, either. Bulger approached a South Boston realtor and said, "Someone hired me to kill you." But, the merciful Bulger said he was willing to settle for a cash payment instead. When afterwards, the terrified realtor arrived at a meeting with Bulger and his enforcers carrying a gun, they beat him viciously. Bulger told his boyos to "go downstairs and get a body bag." He put a pistol to the realtor's head and noted if he put a bullet through the top the skull, the blood loss would be minimal.

Offered a couple of thousand dollars not to do the murder, Bulger told his quarry that amount wouldn't even pay for his cowboy boots. He would only settle for $50,000. Notified, the FBI as usual, did nothing.

The other law enforcement agencies weren't stupid; the local press suggested something was amiss in Bulger's Houdini-like ability to escape from traps; the state, Boston, and DEA personnel began to mistrust the FBI. It came to a head in 1989, when at a Christmas party attended by members of all the area agencies, it was discovered the liquor was from none other than Whitey's South Boston Liquor Mart.

THE NOOSE TIGHTENS

Bulger wound up in the news again when a state trooper caught him in Logan Airport carrying a bag with lumps in it. The trooper noticed the bag, and realized the brick sized lumps were wads of money. This was suspicious indeed. When the trooper tried to stop Bulger, the crime lord handed the bag off to a man who was waiting for him, just as if they were playing football.

The associate went out a revolving door, which Bulger then blocked , and during a shouting and shoving match, prevented the police from following. Bulger was with his girlfriend, Greig, who was carrying $9900—just below the $10,000 threshold where money crossing the border must be declared.

Because of Flemmi and Bulger, and others like them, things continued to go bad so badly for the Mafia, it almost arouses one's pity. The instability of the former Patriarca family was underscored more than ever when in 1989, assassins killed Patriarca's underboss, William Grasso of Connecticut, and attempted to gun "Cadillac" Salemme down in Saugus when he was parking his BMW automobile.

In 1990, the next generation of mobsters who had taken over in Boston from the Angiulo regime were jailed—this time from a bug in the trendy Vanessa's, a restaurant in the Prudential Center in downtown Boston. Flemmi had provided the evidence for the bug there, just as he (and another snitch, Sonny Mercurio) had at the Patriarca initiation ceremony in Medford that brought down the New England mob's leadership in one swoop (See the Patriarca chapter).

Things weren't so bad for Bulger, who like an Irish Mafia Don, delegated most of his dirty work to his lieutenants, shielding himself from responsibility. His new respectability didn't prevent Bulger from threatening a Boston bar owner with a knife. The man happened to be an officer in a mortgage company that denied a $50,000 loan to a drug dealer who owed money to Bulger; while the man was in the back room of the South Boston liquor mart, Bulger swore at him and stabbed liquor boxes with a long knife. The man was willing to testify against Bulger, but as usual, the FBI ignored the opportunity....

Having reached the top, Bulger began to fade from view, becoming in effect, semi-retired. He became so secretive, he was like a bogeyman. People assumed anyone murdered in Southie must have crossed Whitey; those who merely vanished were thought to have crossed Whitey, as well; those who didn't vanish were left wondering if they might at some point cross Whitey. The reputation was great public relations.

Finally, in the early 1990s, the FBI retired Bulger and Flemmi as informants. Connolly claimed the two had decided to pursue legitimate businesses; the reality was, they wanted legitimate fronts to launder their dirty cash. Not long after, in 1992, Bulger made headlines yet again when he suddenly emerged as one of six partners in a $14.6 million lottery ticket. His share of the money would have guaranteed him a hefty income for the rest of his life.

However, the authorities saw it as a thinly disguised attempt to hide the source of his real income. The FBI claimed

Bulger paid out $700,000 himself to buy one sixth of the ticket. Later, when Bulger went into hiding, federal officials made him forfeit this windfall.

But the creaky wheels of justice were now grinding steadily, even if slowly. With the end of Bulger and Flemmi's informer status, authorities made another huge effort to bring them down, working to turn witnesses to testify. That year, 51 men were charged for being part of a drug ring run by Bulger.

There were potential witnesses now. Bulger's old boss, Howie Winter, refused to become an informer and spill the beans on his former lieutenant. "I don't want to be a rat," he said. Winter went to jail again in 1992 for drug peddling; Bulger had greased the track that put him in jail.

Bulger kept receding, leaving Flemmi behind to govern in his name. In 1993, he may or may not have had a local woman's beauty shop riddled with bullets because she was against the expansion of a rooming house owned by a Bulger associate.

It wasn't clear just what the kingpin was up to. Nobody was even sure where Bulger was anymore. In 1994 he reappeared briefly with an associate, then vanished again.

As Bulger had a kingdom of fear, not of love, once he was out of sight, people were no longer compelled to obey him. Authorities made the rounds in jails to ask close lipped prisoners rotting there just what had Whitey done for them to deserve their silence.

The police were fortunate: Bulger was a bad employer. One South Boston native called Paul "Polecat" Moore became frustrated that the high-living Bulger wasn't taking care of his family, which was facing destitution. Deciding he'd been used by the kingpin, he turned evidence. Others, like Burton "Chico" Krantz, a bookmaker, also told the police about having to pay rent to Bulger.

Finally in 1995, the indictments came down against the duo, charging them with extorting money from various drug dealers. The police first arrested Flemmi, who was in a downtown restaurant in Boston. Months later, in Florida, the authorities caught Salemme, hiding at his safe house. Out of seven men indicted for racketeering, Bulger was the only one to remain free.

Allegedly, he heard about the indictments over the radio while he was driving home to Boston, and decided to keep going. Others claimed the FBI had yet again tipped off their star snitch.

But Bulger obviously didn't have the stomach to go on the run by himself. He was originally traveling with his girlfriend Stanley when he found out about the indictments. Letting her off in the classy South Shore suburb of Hingham, he took off with Greig and made her a partner in flight.

One reporter asked Billy Bulger if he was going to tell his brother to give himself in. That idiotic question prompted nothing more than a laugh. He was after all, from Southie, an island off Boston with often the same relationship to the rest of Boston as Sicily has to Italy.

Billy, almost at the same time as Whitey, receded into the shadows, when, facing the end of his dictatorship of the senate, he resigned and took a job running the University of Massachusetts—a job he had absolutely no qualifications for except that he liked to read and had an ability to pad payrolls and give overly-ornate and long-winded speeches.

However, Whitey had prepared for the day of flight, stashing away sums of money all over the country. He had the foresight in 1987 to acquire an Irish passport, which would allow him to roam Europe freely.

Even after he cut his home town loose, the illusion that he was a basically decent criminal-vigilante who took care of his own persisted. In March, 1996, after masked thieves robbed a South Boston Catholic church, not only were the residents shocked, some actually expressed longing for the good old days when Bulger ran the town. People remembered that Whitey usually dealt harshly with such punks, and unlike the police, actually stood for law and order.

"If Whitey was around," said one resident, "this wouldn't have happened."

LIFE ON THE ROAD

During 1995, when many thought he was in Ireland, Whitey was reportedly hiding out in South Boston. He was good at disguises and with his superior acting skills, could successfully imitate a decent law abiding person. For a while, he became Thomas F. Baxter of Selden, New York. The original Baxter was from Woburn, Massachusetts and had died in 1979—presumably without Bulger's assistance. Using Baxter as a front, Bulger obtained a social security card and a driver's license, which he renewed every four years—even while Baxter was still alive!

Out of sight, he was still the same old Whitey. Incensed, and clutching for straws, in October he called up the former FBI section chief, John Morris, at the FBI Academy in Quantico, and said, "You double crossing [expletive]." He also brought up the $7000 he had given Morris. "You took money from me," said Bulger. "If I go to jail, you'll go to jail."

He tried to get Morris to use his "Machiavellian mind" to get the local press to retract stories about him being an informer—Morris had in fact leaked the story to the press about Bulger's stoolie status years earlier. Bulger also accused Morris of having "ruined his life and the lives of his family." Morris said Bulger claimed "I [Morris] also made him a marked man who could be killed for the things I said."

The phone call didn't achieve its objective, and Bulger kept on the move, driving over 65,000 miles in a matter of months.

Apparently as a fugitive, Bulger is more law abiding than ever; he is careful not to attract attention to himself. The landlord in Penny G.'s little town in Louisiana who rented a place to Bulger said Bulger paid his fees in advance, and was clean and articulate. As "Uncle Tom," Bulger showed a humane streak that may or may not have been sincere. He told Penny G. she shouldn't let her children watch violent shows; when fishing, he threw back the small catches. He motivated her husband to start his own business.

Said Uncle Tom/Whitey: "Get off your lazy butt. You've got beautiful kids. You need to make something out of your life." The skills honed running tough street crews from one of the poorest and most desperate urban communities in America was paying off in strange and unexpected ways.

Not everyone was charmed by the kingpin's role as uncle. "He had this attitude like he was the boss," said one male family member. The relative said Whitey was rude, whispering to people in front of him, and even insulting the relative's wife, saying her cooking wasn't as good as Penny's.

Whitey also bragged he didn't have to work—he had others to do that for him, he said. Incensed, the relative challenged Whitey to a pushup contest. The physical fitness fanatic Bulger didn't want to compete, claiming he was the older of the two. The challenger then pulled out his driver's license to compare ages— Bulger refused to follow suit.

Bulger also took an old fashioned view of the sexes, boasting: "I have control of my woman." When he once caught other men eyeballing Greig, he glared at them with that famous Whitey stare and said: "What's the matter? Haven't you ever seen a real woman before?" However, when he went out, Bulger always insisted on occupying dark corners. He also ordered imported beer—was he getting refined in his old age?

He left in July, 1996, returning to Long Island in his Grand Marquis. Not until federal agents came into the scene did Penny G. realize who Uncle Tom really was. So taken in was Penny, she said: "If they're criminals, I don't know which side I'm going on."

The local police chief, who once halted cars downtown to let Bulger cross the road, had a more realistic attitude, one that Bulger would have understood. He said: "I stopped the traffic and let $250,000 get across the street."

Now Bulger has again vanished, possibly under another assumed identity, and the only people who might know where he is are not going to talk. In any case, Bulger is pushing 70, and his career as a crook is over, except as fugitive. He probably has enough money to live till the end of his days—which may be radically curtailed if either the mob or the IRA catches up with him. He is of retirement age, and if he gets sick, he may have problems getting treatment. Having given the FBI a black eye, he can never really relax. He is unable to come home again—or for that matter, be himself again. That is not much of a life; of course that is not much of a consolation to his victims, either.

He seems to have left an indelible impression on his neighborhood. Even in flight, a few old women banded together and bought him a commemorative brick, placed in the sidewalk at the Mary Ellen McCormack development. "He was no angel, but he wasn't as bad as they say," said one of Whitey's benefactors.

However, overall, the community has lost its inflated opinion of their hero; in a recent election, they voted against Billy Bulger's son, who was running for his father's senate seat. Even strong-stomached South Boston had had enough of the brothers Bulger. So annoyed was the neighborhood, someone even carved "WHITEY RAT BULGER" in the paint of a bathroom stall door in Bulger's stronghold of Castle Island.

So what of Whitey? We really only have a few glimpses of him to go by. A cool customer, certainly not loveable—grudgingly respect, perhaps. He is something of a self made man, who in the every day world might have been a corporate executive—or a political leader, like his brother. He is multifaceted: a traitor, murderer, drug distributor, robber, extortionist, sexist and PR genius.

Which raises another question that is more interesting than where he is—that is, who is he? No doubt he could have been many other things, yet he never seems to have had any doubts about what sort of life he wanted—and that was that of a criminal gang leader. But why? Love of evil? The desire to be a big shot in Southie? Boredom? All of the above?

"People all knew him, but nobody knows him," as one acquaintance has pointed out.

Indeed, in a city where, as the poem goes, the Cabots only talk to the Lodges and the Lodges only talk to God, Whitey has only really talked to himself.

Bibliography

(Note: I have used the *Boston Globe*, the *Boston Herald*, and the *Providence Journal Bulletin* and *Providence Evening Bulletin* too copiously to bother giving specific citations)

Abadinsky, Howard, *Organized Crime*, Chicago, Nelson-Hall, Inc., 1990
Adams, Charles Francis, *Chapters of Erie and Other Essays*, New York, Augustus M. Kelley, 1967
"   " *Three Episodes of Massachusetts History*, Boston, Houghton Mifflin, 1896.
Barboza, Joseph, with Hank Messick, *Barboza*, New York, Dell, 1976
Beatty, Jack, *The Rascal King: The Life and Times of James Michael Curley*, Reading, Mass, Addison Wesley Publishing Co., 1992
Becker, Ed, and Charles Rappleye, *All American Mafioso, the Johnny Roselli Story*, New York, Doubleday, 1991

Beschloss, Michael R., *Kennedy and Roosevelt: The Uneasy Alliance*, New York, W.W. Norton, 1980
Beston, Henry, *The Book of Gallant Vagabonds*, New York, Doran Company, 1925.
Bly, Nellie, *The Kennedy Men: Three Generations of Sex, Scandal, and Secrets*, New York, Kensington Books, 1996
Boylan, Brian Richard, *Benedict Arnold, The Dark Eagle*, New York, Norton, 1973
Bulger, William M., *While the Music Lasts*, New York, Houghton Mifflin Company, 1996
Caffrey, Kate, *The Mayflower*, New York, Stein and Day, 1974.
Cameron, Gail, *Rose: A biography of Rose Fitzgerald Kennedy*, New York, G.P. Putnam's Sons, 1971
Canfield, Cass, *Sam Adams's Revolution (1765-1776)*, New York, Harper & Row, 1976
Collier, Peter, and Horowitz, David, *The Kennedys: an American Drama*, New York, Summit Books, 1984.
Connors, Donald F., *Thomas Morton, Twane's United States Authors Series*, Twayne Publishers, Inc., 1969.
Conway, J. North, *New England Women of Substance*, North Attleboro, Mass, Covered Bridge Press, 1996
Cook, Fred J., *Dawn Over Saratoga*, Garden City, Doubleday & Co., 1973
Cressey, Donald R., *Theft of the Nation*, New York, Harper & Rowe, 1969
Curley, James Michael, *I'd do it Again*
Cutler John Henry, *"Honey Fitz"* Indianapolis, Howard Sams & Co.
Davidson, Bill, "How the Mafia Bleeds New England," *Saturday Evening Post*, Nov. 18, 1967
Demaris, Ovid, *The Boardwalk Jungle*, New York, Bantam, 1986
"   " *The Last Mafioso*, New York, Times Books,
Demos, John, "The Maypole of Merry Mount," *American Heritage*, October/November, 1986.
Dineen, Joseph F., *The Kennedy Family*, Boston, Little, Brown, 1959

"   " *The Purple Shamrock: The Hon. James Michael Curley of Boston*, New York, W.W. Norton, 1949
Dorman, Michael, *Payoff: The Role of Organized Crime In American Politics*, New York, David McKay Co., 1972
Draper, Ted, *A Struggle For Power: The American Revolution*, New York, Random House, 1996
Fopiano, Willie, *The Godson*, New York, St. Martin's Press, 1993
Gage, Nicholas, *Mafia, USA*, Chicago, Playboy Press, 1972
"   " *The Mafia is not an Equal-Opportunity Employer*, New York, McGraw-Hill, 1971
Goddard, Donald, *The Insider*, New York, Simon & Schuster, 1992,
Goodwin, Doris Kearns, *The Fitzgeralds and the Kennedys: An American Saga*, New York, Simon & Schuster, New York, 1987
Hamilton, Nigel, *JFK: Reckless Youth*, New York, Random House, 1992
Harlow, Ralph Volney, *Samuel Adams*, Holt, New York, 1923
Hersh, Seymour, *The Dark Side of Camelot*, Boston, Little Brown, 1997
Hoyt, Edwin P., *The Goulds: A Social History*, Weybright and Talley, New York, 1961
"   " *The Damndest Yankees: Ethan Allen and his Clan*, Brattleboro, Vt., Stephen Greene Press, 1976
James, Edward T., editor, *Notable American Women: 1607-1950*, Radcliffe College, 1971
Jackson, Kenneth T. , "Curley," in *Encylcopedia of American Biography*, New York, Harper & Row, New York, 1974
Jeffreys, Diarmuid, *The Bureau: Inside the Modern FBI*, Boston, Houghton Mifflin, 1995
Kessler, Ronald, *The FBI*, New York, Pocket, 1993
"   " *The Sins of the Father:Joseph P. Kennedy and the Dynaasty He Created*, New York, Warner, 1996
Lewis, Paul, *The Grand Incendiary: A Biography of Samuel Adams*, New York, Dial Press, 1973
Lydon, Christopher, "The Sharpest Tool in the Shed," *Boston Book Review* Web site

Nash, Robert Jay, *Bloodletters and Badmen*, New York, M. Evans and Co., Inc., 1991

Madsen, Axel, *Gloria and Joe: The Star Crossed Love Affair of Gloria Swanson and Joe Kennedy*, New York, Arbor House, 1988

Maas, Peter, *The Valachi Papers*, New York, G.P. Putnam's Sons, 1968

Martin, James Kirby, *Benedict Arnold: Revolutionary Hero*, New York, New York University Press, 1997

McCorvey, Klaus, "Sleaze! An Illustrated History," *Boston* magazine Web site

Messick, Hank, *Lansky*, New York, Putnam, 1971

Martin, Ralph G., *Seeds of Destruction, Joe Kennedy and his Sons*, New York, Putnam, 1995

Miller, John C., *Sam Adams, Pioneer in Propaganda*, Stanford, Calif., Standford University Press, 1964

Minnigerode, Meade, *Certain Rich Men*, 1927, New York, G.P. Putnam's Sons

Moore, Samuel Taylor and Sparkes, Boyden, *The Witch of Wall Street: Hetty Green*, Doubleday, New York, 1935

Morison, Samuel Eliot, *Builders of the Bay Colony*, Boston, Houghton Mifflin, 1930.

Morton, Thomas, *New English Canaan*, New York, Burt Franklin, 1967.

O'Connor, Richard, *Gould's Millions*, New York, Doubleday, 1962,

O'Connor, Thomas H., *The Boston Irish*, Boston Northeastern University Press, 1995

O'Neill, Gerard, and Lehr, Dick, *The Underboss: the Rise & Fall of a Mafia Family*, New York, St. Martin's Press, 1989

ONeill, Thomas P., Jr, *Man of the House*, New York, Random House, 1987

Overstreet, Harry and Bonaro, *The FBI in Our Open Society*, 1969

Paine, Lauran, *Benedict Arnold, Hero and Traitor*, New York, Roy Publishers, Inc., 1965

Peterson, Virgil W., *The Mob: 200 Years of Organized Crime in New York*, Ottawa, Ill., Green Hill Publishers, 1983

Reeves, Thomas C., *A Question of Character: A Life of John F. Kennedy*, New York, MacMillan, 1991

Reid, Ed, *The Grim Reapers*, Chicago, Henry Regnery Co., 1969

Roberts, Kenneth, *March to Quebec, Journals of the Members of Arnold's Expedition*, Doubleday, New York, 1938

Ross, Ishbel, *Charmers & Cranks*, New York, Harper & Row, 1965

Russell, Francis, *Adams: An American Dynasty*, New York, American Heritage, 1976

Russell, Francis, *The Great Interlude*, New York, McGraw-Hill, 1964

Scheim, David E, *Contract on America: The Mafia Murder of President John F. Kennedy*, New York, Shapolsky Publishers, Inc., 1988

Sedgewick, John "Blood Brothers," *Esquire*, May 1992

Sifakis, Carl, *American Eccentrics*, New York, Facts on File Publications, 1984

Smith, Page, *The Rise of Industrial America*, New York, McGraw-Hill Book Company, 1984

Swanberg, W.A., *Jim Fisk: the Career of an Improbable Rascal*, New York, Charles Scribner's Sons, 1959.

Taraborrelli, J. Randy, *Sinatra, Behind the Legend*, Secaucus, NJ, Birch Lane Press, 1997

Teresa, Vincent, *My Life in the Mafia*, New York, Doubleday, New York., 1973

"   " *Vinnie Teresa's Mafia*, New York, Doubleday, New York, 1975

Tuchman, Barbara W., *The First Salute: A View of the American Revolution*, New York, Alfred A. Knopf, 1988.

Vanderbilt, Arthur T. II, *Fortune's Children: The Fall of The House of Vanderbilt*, New York: William Morrow and Co., 1989

Vidal, Gore, *Palimpsest*, New York, New York, Random House, 1995

Whalen, Richard J., *The Founding Father: The Story of Joseph P. Kennedy*, New York, The New American Library, 1964,

Zobel, Hiller B. *The Boston Massacre*, New York, Norton, 1970